BLESSINGS

A WomanChrist Reflection on the Beatitudes

D0970031

CHRISTIN LORE WEBER

1817

Harper & Row, Publishers, San Francisco

New York, Grand Rapids, Philadelphia, St. Louis
London, Singapore, Sydney, Tokyo, Toronto

to
John

All Scripture quotations unless otherwise noted are from The Jerusalem Bible, Doubleday and Co., Inc. © 1966, 1967, and 1968 by Darton, Longman & Todd Ltd. and Doubleday & Co., Inc. References noted NAB are taken from The New American Bible, © 1970, Confraternity of Christian Doctrine.

Occasional Scripture references are paraphrased; a "cf." indicates these paraphrases. The working of the Beatitudes is paraphrase from various translations.

BLESSINGS: *A WomanChrist Reflection on the Beatitudes*. Copyright © 1989 by Christin Lore Weber. All rights reserved. Printed in the United States of America. No part of this book may be used or reproduced in any manner whatsoever without written permission except in the case of brief quotations embodied in critical articles and reviews. For information address Harper & Row, Publishers, Inc., 10 East 53rd Street, New York, NY 10022.

FIRST EDITION

Library of Congress Cataloging-in-Publication Data

Weber, Christin Lore.
  Blessings : A WomanChrist Reflection on the Beatitudes/Christin Lore Weber.
    p.   cm.
  ISBN 0-06-254861-1
  1. Beatitudes. 2. Women—Religious life. 3. Spirituality.
I. Title
BT382.W43   1989   88-45993
241.5'3—dc20   CIP

89 90 91 92 93 MCN 10 9 8 7 6 5 4 3 2 1

Contents

Acknowledgments

The people who most influenced the writing of *Blessings* are those who encouraged me at different times in my life to trust my deepest truth. Many of them appear on the pages of this book. They are women and men, adults and children who found gentle or startling ways of bringing me to myself and permitted me in their presence to glimpse the face of God. Among them are Steve and Kathy Callaghan, and Elizabeth—their deep-eyed daughter; Suzanne Swanson; Kath Jesme; Alla Bozarth; Liz and Steve Kensinger and their children; Eva Mapes; and my parents, Alyce and George Lore.

During the long meditation of writing *Blessings* three persons became most essential to the creative process:

John, my spouse, who opened doors to the deepest in me, who encouraged me every day, who first touched the torn oak and predicted the blessing of its flowering.

P.J. Long, who spent many hours with me on the patio in sunshine and by the fire when it rained—who listened, who questioned, who danced the same images for which I was seeking words.

Janice Johnson, my editor at Harper & Row, believed I could write this book even before I began. Without her faith, her encouragement, her eagerness to find each new chapter in the mail, *Blessings* might never have come to be. She is a true "midwife."

I did my research among theologians, feminists, anthropologists, physicists, psychologists; but I found artists most helpful in my attempt to release that deepest truth into words: May Sarton, Anne Truitt, Ursula K. LeGuin, Keri Hulme, Natalie Goldberg, Denise Levertov, and Annie Dillard.

Finally I acknowledge you, Reader. Until you read this book it is only partially complete. The experience and wisdom you bring adds a dimension about which I could not write because it is not mine. Thank you for joining me in reflection and creation. Let us bless one another.

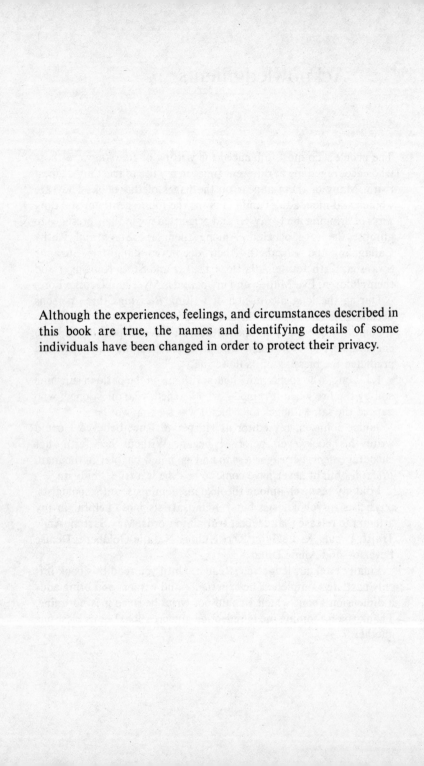

Although the experiences, feelings, and circumstances described in this book are true, the names and identifying details of some individuals have been changed in order to protect their privacy.

FROM THE HEART OF A TORN OAK

On a delicate green day in early February John and I wandered from the path in Briones park and found an ancient oak had fallen, torn apart at its core. Enormous, tangled branches reached out along the ground, half toward the east, half toward the west. John took one route and I took the other—scrambling up to a curved branch twice my height from the ground. Sitting there I took in the warmth of the sun and the vision of the mountain on the horizon. John stood for a while on an upward-leaning branch, and then came down to examine the radical wound that scarred this magnificent tree creature.

"It must have been a great wind."

He reverently touched and traced the tree's silvered age lines. Then he bent to where the centermost root of the tree had been anchored into the ground and smoothed the earth with his hand.

"No one has touched this earth for hundreds of years. When a giant tree like this splits it must make a terrible tearing sound."

Then, touching more closely into the oak's core, formed those many hundreds of years ago, he mused, "Carbon. There must have been a fire when she was very young. The new growth encased the wound until she grew too large, or until the wind blew too strong . . . Even though she's torn in two, she has some connection with her roots. Maybe there's enough so she'll have leaves in the spring."

He lifted me down from my perch; we stood a few more moments in the presence of the torn oak, and then left her.

But today I have returned. On this day, when I begin to reflect and write about living a WomanChrist spirituality, I am drawn back to Briones park. I am drawn to the place where creation whispers a blessing from the heart of a torn oak, upon whose fallen branches burst the fragile, unlikely leaves of spring.

WomanChrist spirituality brings together and reconciles the most fundamental opposites known to traditional patriarchal Christianity: Woman and the Christ. All the dualisms originate here— that the Christ is a man. The living heart of creation tears apart at its core as a result of our pitiful misunderstanding. We are torn even at the center of our selves. We live, but without the power of life, for the power arises from intercourse with what we have come to experience as the "other," the "opposite."

The blessing of WomanChrist spirituality is precisely this intercourse. The blessing of WomanChrist spirituality is reconciliation of Woman with the Christ, and by this union the healing of the many dualisms that have torn at our lives for centuries. Perhaps the best-kept secret of Christianity is that the Christ and Sophia (Divine Feminine Wisdom) are one. Even Paul writes to the people of Corinth that Christ is the Wisdom (Sophia) of God (1 Cor. 1:25).

When we believe that opposites stand against each other, we create a dangerous illusion. From such an illusion comes limited vision, cutthroat competition, discrimination against those we believe are different, and war of all kinds—within ourselves, within the family, between communities and nations.

If we believed instead that opposites exist within each other as catalysts for the release of creative power, we could change our whole outlook on reality. We would enlarge our souls. What we presently exclude to keep ourselves safe from questions, we would begin to include in a daring acceptance of possibilities. We would expand our world. We would finally be able to love. And that is the point: to love everything, and to love it into total being.

The way of blessing by which opposites are reconciled and the world is expanded is articulated in the Beatitudes of St. Matthew's Gospel (5:3–10). Each Beatitude is an act of faith in the radical potential of our world to be made whole. Each is a kind of koan, a paradox of seemingly irreconcilable opposites that plunges one's soul into a meditative quest for wholeness. And each Beatitude is a blessing that graces us to incarnate its promise of unity.

I have always found the Beatitudes both beautiful and mysterious but never so much as when I listened to Paul Winter's *Missa Gaia* while driving along the wild and primal north shore of Lake Superior. Winter's music infused the ancient words of blessing with new power for me, inviting me to listen in a more profound way. The blessings of this book echo the music of *Missa Gaia,* which became for me, that day, a sacrament of union between the feminine mystery of Gaia (Earth) and the masculine mystery of the Word. We call that union Christ, who is our Incarnate Blessing.

Each Beatitude, each blessing, contains such a paradox and gives us a way to live WomanChrist spirituality, a way to mend the tear in the fabric of creation. The Beatitudes reveal the Way of Christ. They are not laws to be obeyed, but blessings to be contemplated and incarnated. If we approach their meaning through analysis we will fail to understand them. Instead we need to receive them with love, as the seed is received, and hold them within us until they bear fruit in our lives. We cannot explain them; but we can tell stories about finding them enfleshed in the people and situations we encounter.

Each Beatitude contains power within itself. It becomes the Word in us being made Flesh. Each Beatitude is the Divine Egg from which WomanChrist comes to be. Our lives develop out of the paradox of beatitude until each of us becomes an incarnation of its blessing.

"There comes a time in our lives when we seek out our opposite to love," says my friend Judith, while we sip our peppermint tea. "I don't think we can escape it, we need that person desperately; for no one else has the power to call forth what is necessary to our completion as human beings. All spirituality leads here. All life, too, if we are true and truly *want* to live fully."

When my Grandpa Klimek died my Grandma sobbed until she couldn't speak. I was eight years old. I had wandered back to the bedroom from the parlor where Grandpa lay in his simple wooden coffin. Grandma sat looking in her brass-framed mirror, watching her tears slide uncontrollably down her cheeks. When the sobs subsided she picked up her music box, wound it, and lifted the cover. As the melody played, her sobs rose like a wail from somewhere so deep that even I could sense the agony.

I was confounded. Why would she cry? I never thought they even *liked* each other. His temper was swift, her smoldering anger was long. He was always playing when she needed his help, and she was forever too busy with serious matters to play.

I can see myself as I was, the small child unnoticed at the entryway to her grandmother's unconsolable grief. And, listening through the child's ears, I know the sound the ancient oak tree made when it was sundered by some enormous wind. And I begin to sense the secret hidden in her torn heart.

A Gift of Welcome

Blessed are the poor in spirit,
theirs is the fullness of heaven.

THE STRANGER'S SONG

Damp wisps of white hair escaped from the large, tight braid wound into a crown, laurel-leaf fashion, around Beth's head. She and Josie sat in caned-seat maple rockers on the large screened porch three flights up from the alley over the back of Anderson's Hardware in Minneapolis, Minnesota, fanning themselves and singing hymns. I knocked.

"Welcome!" Beth smiled. "Come in, girl, come in out of the heat before you faint dead away. July has been an oven this year, but we've some shade here on the porch and it catches a wee bit of breeze too.

"Josie, go pour the girl a glass of lemonade."

I opened the screen door and stepped onto the porch and into Beth's life.

"There, now you look a bit more comfortable. That heat can fairly do a person in. Would you like to sit for a spell and visit? Sing some hymns with us? We'd like to know your name and what it was that brought you to our door."

I was a stranger. That was the summer I had lost my job, the summer I hadn't money enough to complete the master's program at the university, the summer of my father's heart attack and my mother's breast cancer. Two weeks before I had moved from my apartment because I could no longer afford it, and had gone to live temporarily with a friend.

Another friend had given me a part-time job visiting the elderly poor in a deteriorating urban neighborhood that had been bought up by a developer and scheduled for demolition as soon as all the properties were vacated. Only the old people were left; they were too poor and too infirm to find anywhere else to go, and politics prevented the developers from evicting them.

My responsibility was to assure that the dilapidated properties were still occupied—that some poor old person hadn't died, unnoticed. What I actually found myself doing was visiting with lonely elders of the community who had become strangers in their own neighborhood—to one another, and even to themselves.

Some of the people awaited the visit eagerly. They met me at the door with photo albums and stories of ocean voyages from the "old country," of wild times on Hennipen Avenue during Prohibition, of visiting the family farm up by St. Cloud. I turned page after page of albums filled with sepia-colored pictures of serious women, dapper men, and stark houses set in rolling Minnesota prairie.

Others were not so pleased. They associated me with all they had lost. I represented the developers who had bought their property, stolen their dignity, and were awaiting their deaths.

My foot sank through the rotting boards on the steps of one of the houses on my list of properties. I knocked on the screen door. A vicious dog snarled at me and bared his teeth. His long hair was matted with filth that clattered along the floor like beads when he ran to the door. An old woman with vacant eyes grumbled from the corner of the living room, where she sat in front of a black-and-white television.

"Who's 'at?" she grumbled.

I told her my name and why I had come.

"I dunwanna see ya," she mumbled, "cancha see I'm busy?"

But she got up anyway, locked the dog in the kitchen in back, and let me in. She gestured toward an old man lying on a dirty cot.

"He's sick," she shrugged, "No feet no more. Nobody gives a damn. Bes' thing ta do is jis watch TV."

The whole house stank of gangrene, dog filth, and garbage that littered the floor and most of the furniture. "Doesn't the health department send someone to care for your husband?"

"Yeah. But I don' let 'em in no more. Fancy goddamn nurse says we gotta git ridda the dog. But who's gonna protect us from them no 'count kids if we ain't got no dog? Tell me that, wouldja? Could git killed in this 'ere neighborhood if ya ain't gotta dog ta scare 'em off."

She turned again to stare at her soap opera. A sultry and spoiled young woman pouted to her husband because he wouldn't buy her the new car she wanted. The old woman dismissed me from her attention. I couldn't stand the pain, the desperation, the stench, the sound of the dog growling and throwing himself against the kitchen door. I said good-bye and went away. I never returned there. I didn't have the courage.

This was the job that brought me to Beth's door. "Poverty isn't pretty," she said when I told about this experience. "It isn't romantic. It takes away that something that makes us human. That man and woman are poor. I'm not poor. I don't have much, but I'm not poor."

She loved telling her story. Many years ago—"Long, long before you were born, dear"—Beth lived in "the old country" within the circle of a loving and pious family.

"I was a beautiful young woman; my hair fell long and gold as the sunshine over my shoulders. My eyes sparkled bluer than the dancing stream on my father's farm and my skin was soft and the color of rich cream. I was brimming with love. Love of the earth and the sky, of my family, and of the young man. No wonder he wanted to marry me. So we were engaged and I dreamed of our life together and of our children and their children for generations.

"Then I was given a greater love. A Voice called to me. Clear. As clear as you can hear me now. *'Go to America.'* What? What's in America, I wondered. *'You are needed in America,'* the Voice gently insisted. And its insistence came into me like love itself—like the sweetest and the deepest, warmest light. The Voice *was* Love—stronger than any other love in my life: the love of my family, of my country, or even of my young man. And so I packed my trunk and took a steamer to America.

"*I* didn't know what I was doing. I had no idea how *big* this place would be, how confusing. I knew no one. I couldn't speak the language. What good was I?

"Then Love led me to a church. There a missionary woman took me under her wing, taught me English, and let me join her in her travels across this great country, preaching the word of Love wherever people would listen, stopping wherever we might be needed to help out—the old, the poor, the sick. Oh, it was a full, full life. Oh, girl, I could tell you such stories!

"Finally—I was still a young woman, mind you—Love brought me here to Minneapolis and put it into the heart of old Mr. Anderson to let me live above his hardware store. I worked in there part time to earn my rent and the bit I needed for food and clothes.

"Well, there was plenty of Love needed here, let me tell you!"

Josie chimed in, then, to tell how Beth took the poor and destitute and drunk men and women of the inner-city streets into her home one by one. She gave them food, clothes, and a place to rest and get well. Her only requirement was that they stop drinking. She had loved people in this welcoming, healing, simple, and magnanimous way for forty-five years.

Josie had been one of the people Beth had "saved." "I was a woman of the streets," she said. "One night I was passed out on a corner when Beth came by. She picked me up—Beth was still strong then, not shaky with the Parkinson's, like now—and took me to her place above the store.

"But I couldn't take the rule about the drinking. When I had slept off my hangover, I dressed and went back to the bar. Well, I was sitting there with a bunch of the guys, being rowdy and getting a good buzz on, when Beth came storming through the door, her blue eyes blazing!

"She came right up to the bar stool where I was sitting, nursing a whiskey sour, and in a loud voice she said, 'Josie, you are ruining your life. You can stay here and die, or come with me. I will give you a home and good, honest, loving work to do.' Then Beth laid her hand on my head. At her touch I felt something like an electric shock go clean through me. I was so surprised I fell right smack off that bar stool.

"I went with Beth that day, and I've been with her ever since."

Beth welcomed all who came to her, and her welcome communicated the power of that Love she once heard calling her. She and Josie no longer live above Anderson's Hardware. The whole area has been renovated, and the hardware store, redesigned, contains bright fabrics, handcrafted pottery, silver jewelry, and bright imports from around the world. The inner city at the intersection of Madison and Grand has become a pretty classy place.

It is fifteen years since last I saw Beth and Josie. Perhaps both have died. But Beth continues her life in everything she welcomed, everyone she loved. I know I welcome the presence of her memory within me.

I do know that Beth never stopped hearing the Voice of Love. Josie whispered one day in confidence that her friend often knelt all night in her bedroom listening to Love's music. And I know Love sang to her, because of a conversation we once had.

"Beth," I confided, "what can I do with my life? I don't know who I am or what I can contribute. I can't find God anymore."

"Listen," she smiled.

"I try, but I don't hear."

"Don't try!"

I must have looked perplexed, because she laughed at me—hard. Then she tapped her finger on my forehead and said again, "Don't try. Just clear all the stuff out of your attic. When you are empty and clean the Song will begin. The bird, the Holy Songster, she will begin to sing then. And, oh, the beauty of her Song. Then you will hear and you will never stop listening and you will desire only the Song."

Beth closed her eyes. Her relaxed face looked ancient and young. I knew she was listening.

BEFRIENDING THE STRANGER

Holy Mystery stands at the door and knocks. Beth welcomed the stranger without fear, while just down the street another old woman feared the stranger so intensely that she seemed to have estranged herself from everything lifegiving. The Mystery standing as a stranger at the door of our lives also stands at the doorway to our deepest self. There we encounter the most fearsome stranger of all—and the most intimate friend.

These opposites live within us: images of our selves, images of the world, images of the Holy One. We perceive this image as friendly, that image as threatening and fearsome. We turn from what seems threatening; we ignore that image as most of the passersby ignored the person wounded on the road to Jericho. Only another stranger, a person from foreign Samaria, was willing to confront the danger of the road, the danger of the unknown, to recognize a kinship with the wounded, strange one.

"Who is my neighbor?" query those constantly testing the wisdom of Jesus. "Whom must I befriend?" The answer, of course, is the stranger . . . the dangerous one. And only the part of me who is also the stranger can bend to the danger and welcome it in another. I who am the stranger befriend the stranger in another, in the world, in the Holy One.

The stranger walks the road with us unrecognized because the stranger belongs to the future. The stranger forms at the boundaries of the personal or universal cosmos as an image of probability. When we befriend the stranger we embrace the probable and give it reality.

We fear the stranger because we resist change. We try to control the unknown. But we who conceive probability in the darkness of unknowing bring forth hope. Women crouch in a birthing position at the edge of this known world to bring forth the stranger. What we do in our bodies we do first in our souls; and what we do in our souls affects everything. Our God is a woman bringing forth the stranger. And, by embracing and befriending each new form of life, She expands creation.

"I have become a stranger to myself," a woman confided to me after the death of her husband. "As the months wear on I know less and less of who I am, but at the same time I am surprised constantly by an awakening in myself of desires and inclinations I never knew I possessed."

The inner stranger makes her presence known all the time, but most strongly as the result of some emptying, some poverty of spirit. Into the emptiness possibility flows, and we are simultaneously exhilarated and disoriented. If the emptiness comes as the result of some tremendous loss—the death of a loved one, the loss of a home of many years, the decision of growing children to move from the family in which they were reared, the long absence of a friend—then the appearance of the inner stranger can feel like a confirmation of the loss and a betrayal of grief.

At such a time we teeter on the edge of possibility. The strange faces of the unknown rise from the depths. Will we welcome them, befriend them, incarnate them? We must choose. If we fear too much, we risk the plight of the old woman who set her vicious dog against the incoming stranger. Fear made her indiscriminate. All strangers were harmful, even those who could have healed her pain.

If we choose to befriend a stranger who is too new and different from what we have known, we risk the loss of all by which we identified ourselves in the past. Like Beth, when we follow the new Voice we could be agreeing to leave our land, our families, and our beloved. When our worlds expand, the old structures of soul and relationship that we considered so solid seem to crumble.

The first time I saw Irish farmhouses I was struck with an apt metaphor for what happens to our past as we expand the boundaries of the new: The houses on these ancient but still operative farms are made of stone from the land. Ordinarily there are four or five stone buildings on one farm, usually set in a row, and in varying states of repair.

"You notice the big house, there," explained my Irish friend, "that one is where the family lives now. But do you see next to it that somewhat run-down house that has no windows anymore? They lived there maybe fifty years ago. Now look at the others, tumbled down almost. And finally, see that pile of stones there with moss and vines growing round them? That was the first house.

"Now you may wonder," she continued, "why they leave the stones there—and you may wonder why they don't reuse the same stones for the new house when the old is no longer usable. It is because of the spirits, you see. The spirits of all the people and everything that happened in that house enter into the stones when the people leave. It is a sacred place. The only thing to be done is to allow the stones to return to the earth. The spirits then will rest."

In the same way the stranger within us, befriended, does not take the place of who we formerly were, but expands the totality of our identity. Although we no longer live out of who we were before, that person is never gone, and the spirit inhabits the place where she continues to be. I am who I was, who I am, and who I will be. I am all of myself simultaneously. I am all the myriad of possibilities. I am infinite strangers awaiting welcome and incarnation. I am always both the stranger and the friend who, when they enclose each other, widen the world.

When we sense the presence of the Mysterious Stranger, we might pray:

> Constant Movement of life,
> Breath of ever-changing being,
> Holy One, forming and transforming continually—

This dancing world is Your Body,
This evolving world is Your being flung forth;
Let me trust the changing of my own life,
For I have become a stranger in a strange land.
   In the disappearance of the familiar
      Let me recognize the mystery of Your transforming
      dance;
   In the preponderance of the untried
      Let me accept the challenge of your unfolding
      newness;
   In the absence of old friends
      Let me discover the presence of the human circle;
   In the landscape of the strange
      Let me open to the wonder of earth.
Your being in me turns in a kaleidoscope of brilliance
And darkness opens into light that dazzles then dims.
Everything given, give me courage to let go,
Then hold me safe in the emptiness,
As the changing suffuses my life
And brings me forth
New.

WELCOMING THE WORLD

Each self is a microcosm of the world. When we look out into this larger sphere we often see reflected there all we have befriended and all we have estranged in our individual selves. There is nothing that is not a part of each of us. Everything is connected.

If I fear or hate the stranger within me, I will fear or hate the stranger she resembles in the world. These world strangers may be individuals or groups of people, particular types of experiences, certain places or events—anything in the process of creation that represents what is new and might or might not become incarnate. When I fear or hate the stranger, then the stranger continues to be estranged. The unbefriended stranger splits creation and hinders or actually distorts the creative process. WomanChrist spirituality seeks to reconcile the opposites, befriend the stranger in everything, and enhance the creative process in the world.

The stranger is never evil in itself. But our hatred and fear can give a kind of power to the stranger that, when reflected back upon us, feels destructive. We recoil from the reflection of our own hatred and fear. Repudiation of any facet of the self tears and divides the vital core of the soul. The division we cause in creation by alienating the stranger rends not only our individual souls but the soul of the world at the very core of power from which life proceeds.

I need to ask myself who in this world is the stranger to me and who is the friend: the poor? the rich? liberals? conservatives? atheists? churchgoers? Communists? the military? peace activists? intellectuals? workers? the old? the young? men? women? homosexuals? heterosexuals? those in authority? those of a different race or nationality? those who work a lot? those who play a lot? artists? entrepreneurs?

Which experiences will I accept: aggression? peace? hunger? pleasure? silence? sound? activity? solitude? poverty? wealth? power? commonness? simplicity? complexity? responsibility? spontaneity? illness? health? perfection? error? death?

How can I befriend them all? Somehow I must. We must alienate nothing. Our alienation gives the stranger the power to destroy us. Collective alienation of a world stranger gives it the power to destroy the world. Rather we must circle the stranger with love and recognize the friend whom the stranger conceals. Befriending the stranger reveals a friend only love can see.

A friend of mine, who has for many years been active in the world peace movement, spoke recently of her chagrin over protests she made in the past against people and groups who opposed her point of view. All at once she has realized that those who promote aggression as a way to bring peace and prevent war are not the enemy. *It is the estrangement of aggression from peace that brings war.* She has recognized that she has been aggressive in the cause of peace, and that aggression is a powerful breakthrough of energy to achieve a goal. It can be wonderfully creative, and is in fact operative in every creative act. But we have so estranged aggression that many of us associate it only with war. Only by going to war, by setting up an "other" as enemy, can we now exercise aggression. Aggression and war have become identified.

"Justice and peace shall kiss," sings the psalmist (Psalm 85:11 NAB). When I was a small girl, growing up during World War II, that line evoked for me the image of two women, Justice and Peace. Justice always held a sword sharpened on both sides; one edge was called Mercy, the other edge Truth. Her face was determined, her stance strong. She had braided her long hair and wound it into a crown. She wore a deep violet jerkin and a cape of silver. Her goal was to end war forever. Peace wore her hair long and crowned it with flowers. It flowed free down the back of her long white dress. She was a dancer with welcoming eyes and slender arms, and hands in which she held a ray of pure golden light. As the two women kissed, the light and the sword fused and became one.

I lived in Omaha, Nebraska, at the time. Because of the many military installations there, the population often experienced enemy alerts—blackouts. Although I was not yet five years old I was vitally conscious of the war. Each day my father went to an aircraft factory to help construct B-29s for the war effort. My uncle Peter wrote occasionally from the South Pacific, where he was a private pilot for Admiral Nimitz, and my mother and father talked often of his frontline view of the war.

But the most frightening and most real lessons of war were the blackouts. Sirens blew all over the city and the lights went out. My mother turned off every light in the apartment and held me close, cuddled on her lap, as military planes droned over our heads. We were not supposed to know if it was a drill or if the bombers above were those of the enemy. I remember the fear clutching at my stomach. To calm myself I closed my eyes and imagined Justice and Peace embracing, kissing, while the sword of Mercy and Truth became one with the light.

WomanChrist spirituality invites us to discover, recover, or create ways to embrace the stranger in every situation of life. No one can tell us how to do this, for each of us is responsible for that welcoming and that embrace that are needed in our particular life and surroundings. And the form of welcome must fit the nature of the estrangement.

Joanna feared for a friend of hers who had been taken as a hostage in Lebanon. We spoke about it recently following the man's return to the United States. "At first," Joanna reflected, "I prayed very hard for his release. Those who had captured him seemed vague to me—wicked, evil men who were the enemy. But as time went on I began to realize that they were people too, people struggling for freedom in their homeland, people who did not want to die but were willing to give their lives in a struggle to bring justice to the world as they knew it.

"So I began to send them peace in a prayer from the deepest places of my soul. I imagined them being wrapped in peace as if in glowing light; and I felt myself to be in a very strong sympathy with them. When my friend was released it seemed to me that I had had a part in it. I suppose that was pretty egocentric of me, a little grandiose, but I wanted to take some credit for the peaceful resolution to a very frightening situation for everyone concerned."

Joanna *was* an intimate participant in the hostage affair. She became the meeting point, the agent of welcome, the befriender. Within her own soul she recognized herself as both the hostage and the hostage-taker; the terrorized and the terrorist. She became all three: imprisoning, imprisoned, and released.

WomanChrist is the meeting point of stranger and friend wherever in ourselves or in the world they have been separated. Living a WomanChrist spirituality commits us to accept our connections, even those that frighten us because of the creative changes they imply. Everything that happens in creation affects me. And everything I do, every decision I make, everything I embrace, everything I estrange affects the whole. Nothing can be strange unless I make it so; and when I do I enter into an illusion. Everything I alienate in creation I have first alienated within myself. I cannot reject the one without the other. I am the stranger I have turned away. I am the enemy. The war is within.

Let us pray:

> O Holy One of Welcome,
> You who know so well
> And hold so tenderly
>> The bird fallen from the nest,
>> The flower crushed underfoot,

The wheat plagued by drought,
The small boat tossed upon the waves,
The child blind from birth,
The old woman forgetful of her daughter's name,
The friend speaking false without thought,
The lover absorbed in her own pain,
The teacher caught in ignorance,
The leader afraid to step out into tomorrow,
Embrace me today.
Keen is the pain of my life's flaw,
Awful, the tear in this fabric of Your creation,
Lonely, this stranger I have made of the world and of myself.
Flow through the rip in my soul with Your healing Love;
In the emptiness of my heart sing Your Creation Song
Of Welcome.

BLESSED ARE THE POOR IN SPIRIT

Women know about emptiness. The emptiness of the womb, the emptiness of letting go: of the child being born, of the adolescent forming her own feelings and ideas, of the young adult leaving home, of the spouse seeking his own way. The immense vastness of the soul is feminine, as is the vast emptiness of cosmic space. Within each vastness creation choreographs her intricate dance. Within each vastness the Stranger of God, that dark and unrecognized feminine in the Holy, rises and seeks an invitation to the dance.

Blessed are the poor in spirit. Happy are those who respect the vastness of womansoul, who have kept a space for the stranger and for the Stranger of God.* Blessed are the empty, the womanwombs

---

* I develop the image of the "Stranger of God" in *WomanChrist* (San Francisco: Harper & Row, 1987), chapter 6.

ready to receive, to conceive, to enflesh, to continue the creation in the dance of cells, in the dance of possibilities, in the embrace of what is strange, of what is new, of what is unknown and untried.

Blessed are the poor in spirit who have been emptied by the workings of life upon them. Blessed are those who have lost whatever filled them up, whatever stopped the dance by limiting the vastness.

Paradox reconciles the opposites. Heaven—fullness—is drawn into creation by poverty of spirit—vastness, emptiness.

Heaven flows into the vastness. Infinite possibility swells up in the emptiness. Once we recognize that we *are* the creation, we *are* the vastness, we *are* the space for the Divine Dance of Being, we *are* the cosmic womb in which All-That-Is constantly births itself, then nothing possible will be strange.

A woman who came to me for spiritual guidance told the story of a spirituality group in which she and her husband had participated for two years. They had long been involved in religious and spiritual discussion groups and wanted the experience of this new group to be somewhat different from those of the past. They came up with the idea of taking each of the Beatitudes and living its blessing for three months, sharing with the group the stories arising from the experience.

They were transformed. Each of them, the woman told me, became aware of realities in life never before expected. They committed themselves to goals unthinkable in the past, and made the commitment happily—with beatitude, blessing. One volunteered two days a week in a shelter for battered women; another began to participate actively in the peace movement. A doctor donated an evening a week at a clinic. But it was not *what* each of them did that was important; it was that the commitment was uncharacteristic of them as they had always thought of themselves. Receiving a Beatitude into the soul with the intention of incarnating it in life had led each person to befriend a stranger and thereby to heal one of creation's wounds.

The stranger's blessing comes to the person who is poor in spirit, the person who can befriend with simplicity and magnanimity.

Beth welcomed me into her home and offered me refreshment before she even knew my name—while I was still a stranger to her.

Probably she had always been so welcoming. Her simplicity provided her with an instinct toward the stranger resembling that of Jesus, who could see into the hearts of all who approached him. Simplicity is a condition of soul that recognizes, accepts, and honors the individual's continuity with the totality of creation. Simplicity says, "Everything is an aspect of the whole. All is One."

Simplicity incarnates the vast emptiness. What do I touch when I touch the thin green leaf of spring? What moves within my fruitful womanbody, part and notpart of me? To whom do I give food and drink when I receive a guest? What smiles in the smile I give, and who receives? Simplicity says the smile, the one smiling, and she who receives are one.* I have nothing to give, so simplicity is required, a simplicity of oneness with the vast creative act. I have no thing to give: I am the gift; and whatever seems to be given—food, or drink, or smile—is one with me. I am the gift whose nature is to be given by the One Who Is. The whole vast universe is the outpouring of the Holy One. I, too, am poured out, as is the stranger. We are one in that outpouring. Together we are the gift. Together we are one. Our condition of life is simplicity.

Simplicity unites the strangers. Woman with the Christ. WomanChrist.

WomanChrist is the outpouring through the vastness, the heaven flowing up through the poor in spirit. I have and am no *thing,* I am the focus of the fullness of life swelling up in the vast womb of creation. I am WomanChrist. I can afford to be magnanimous in my simplicity.

Once I took five adolescent girls to visit with Beth. At the time I was directing the pastoral care department in a large treatment center for emotionally disturbed children in Minneapolis. These particular girls had grown up in families at the upper end of the economic scale. They had had plenty of money, but not enough love. Two of them had run away from their homes to become teenage prostitutes on Hennepin Avenue. The police found them and brought them to the shelter attached to the center. The other three

---

* I am indebted to Bernadette Roberts for this image developed in *The Experience of No-Self* (Boulder, CO: Shambhala Publications, 1984), 65.

girls each felt rejected by her family, bored with school, angry with life, lost and hopeless.

I explained to them what I knew about Beth's life, and they agreed to visit the old woman. We drove to the corner of Madison and Grand, parked the van, and climbed the three flights from the alley to Beth's apartment. Josie answered the door.

"Beth has not been well," she smiled gently, "but she didn't want to cancel the visit. She has been looking forward to meeting the girls."

We went into the living room, where Beth sat on her rocker with a colorful afghan covering her legs. She smiled radiantly and invited us to sit around her. With no preliminaries, Beth asked each girl to identify herself. Then, calling each girl by name, she uttered a kind of prophecy over her.

"Sara, you have been given great gifts of intelligence. Use them. Within you is power. So far you have used it selfishly, and it has gotten you into a mighty lot of trouble. But you can use it for good. You *will* use it for good. I trust you will."

Somehow she managed to touch a very secret place in each girl. This intimate knowledge of their souls seemed to them akin to magic. When Beth had finished the girls were mesmerized.

"I have a gift for you," Beth smiled. "It is only a little thing, but I want you to know by it that I love you with a very special love and that I will love you forever. I believe in you—that each of your lives will be beautiful and good."

Then she gave each of them a crisp dollar bill clipped to a card on which a verse from the Gospels was printed.

We went down the stairs in silence and climbed into the van. "But she is poor," remarked an amazed Sara, "she couldn't afford five dollars. I am going to keep this dollar bill all my life." There was silence among the girls for a few moments, then Sara spoke again. "We were strangers to her. How did she know us so well, and how could she love us so much?"

THE LIVING GIFT

Through the vast channel called poverty of spirit a gift flows toward the stranger and friend alike. It is the gift that creates, sustains, and strengthens the bond by which the welcomed stranger becomes the friend. Poverty of spirit also compels the gift into itself so that the giver is in turn gifted in her giving.

The giving of gifts has ancient roots in womanculture and we need to recognize how great a role this activity plays in women's spirituality. As in any practice of spirituality, gift giving has its origin at the foundation of being itself and is a common part of our everyday lives. Although it naturally produces a transformational energy, it can be distorted by egocentricity to become destructive to individuals and the community.

When I look around my office today I notice that much of what is contained here came to me as a gift. An almost-blue alabaster bird caught open-throated in song sits atop the stereo speaker. He (I have always thought of this bird as "he") came to me as a gift from Marti, a sensitive girl I taught in the mid-1960s when she was in high school and I was a new teacher. So far no one I have known has needed this bird more than I, so he stays with me. Perhaps someday I will feel the gift energy in him rising and needing to move on and I will give him away, as I did a lustrous carved-bone bird from Korea given to me by Jeannette. When I moved from Minnesota my sister exclaimed that she had always loved the subtly beautiful thing, so that bird became a gift again.

Next to the bird is a carved soapstone vase, which my mother brought as a gift from Phoenix. It holds six shafts of wheat given to me from a funeral spray of flowers by the wife of a friend who had died. Draped on the wall is a handwoven wool rug made by a woman in Peru, who gave it to my friend Liz when she visited there. Some years later Liz gave the rug to my first spouse, Pat, who gave it to me.

Here is a rainbow candle from Kathy. There is a carved rosewood mother-and-child statue from Pat, who had received it as a gift from a priest at the St. Paul Seminary, who had received it from the artist; a leather box from Mary, who had received it from her Uncle George before he died. And next to it a smooth oval leather container from Mimi, who had received it from her husband, who had received it from his mother—in it is frankincense from Sister Bernadette of the Poor Clare Monastery in Minneapolis.

I can't believe how much there is! The rocking chair: The old man made it from walnut trees he had planted the year he married, and cut down the year his wife died to make seven rockers—six for his children, and this one for a gift to a stranger. The holy water font my great-grandmother Johanna received as a gift for her first communion and brought to America with her. She gave it to her son, Anton, who gave it to his wife, Elizabeth, my grandmother, who gave it to my mother, who gave it to me.

And that is just in *this* room.

Each of the gifts seems alive with a kind of power connected still with its many givers and with the possibility of its being given again to someone else in the continuous movement that is the essence of gift. This gift bestows on us more than the object given. It endows both giver and receiver with its power. The noun is transformed into a verb. The gift becomes a gifting in which both giver and receiver are gifted. The least complex movement of gifting is between two people, back and forth; but the most creative movement is circular, among many. In circular gifting the gift moves, not back and forth, but always to a third person, so that gifting creates community.

When my first spouse died, Ray and Maggie lavished gifts upon me. Their secure and loving presence kept the world together during preparations for the funeral and for the tenuous weeks following. They literally kept me alive—making sure I had food, that my house was safe (Ray put locks on my windows), that my bills were paid. After a month or so of receiving their totally generous giving, I expressed my growing concern that I would never be able to repay them.

"Someone else will," they smiled gently. "You have given like this to others. Others have given to us in the past. Someday we will be in need, and someone will be there to provide. That will repay us.

What we have given you, you will give another. The gift continues."

The gift that stops, dies. The gift we hold onto possessively fills us up, destroying that poverty of spirit that draws gift into itself, *through* itself, assuring its continual movement and thus its energy and life. With each giving the gift increases in value and power. We recognize this with such gifts as family heirlooms. I know, for example, that I will someday give my great-grandmother's holy water font to my sister's daughter, Krista; and that when it becomes a gift to her it will have increased in value from what it is now. This value has no monetary significance; its significance comes from the life energy of those who have assured that it continues to be a gift.

The realm of gift is vastly different from the realm of commerce.* We feel a sense of violation when someone *sells* that which was given as a gift. The value of gift differs from the value associated with "profit." The gift bonds us to another. Selling a gift symbolically severs the bond it represents and drains the gift itself of its significance. What would have happened to my relationship with Ray and Maggie if, when I asked how I could every repay them, they had said: "Well, our time is worth $40 an hour and we spent upwards of 80 hours taking care of your needs, so $3,200 would be an appropriate payment."

Another distortion that often affects the spirituality of gift giving is giving for the purpose of getting something in return. This is not gifting at all, but commerce. In politics we call it bribery. In our day-to-day lives, however, and within the context of our relationships, this distortion can be so subtle as to fool us into mistaking it for true gift giving.

A client of mine once referred to this as "deal making." She had discovered the deal-making tendency within herself and was beginning to realize the problems it had caused her. "It's like I am constantly making deals," she explained. "Inside I am saying, 'I will do this for you, then you will have no choice but to like me and return some similar gift.' But the problem is that the other person knows nothing of the deal I'm making; so I am always left with a terrible

---

* The essence of these notions about gift giving has been culled from Lewis Hyde's *The Gift: Imagination and the Erotic Life of Property* (New York: Random House, 1983).

feeling of being cheated. I'm just now understanding that the person who is doing the cheating is *me*."

Some of us spend enormous amounts of time in shopping centers buying "gifts" for others, when what we are really doing is attempting to make a deal for their friendship and good feeling toward us. This distortion of gifting is subtle, insidious, and destructive of the soul. It arises from egocentricity rather than from the poverty of spirit through which the true movement of gifting flows. It is a manipulation of the gift-giving process for the purpose of being filled, oneself. It is a violation.

True gifting requires trust. The process is one of relinquishing control. The gift, by its nature, moves toward the greatest emptiness, the deepest poverty of spirit. To let it go means emptying myself, losing control of the gift and of the power to make the receiver "pay me back." I simply must trust that my own emptiness will draw a new gift into itself, and that the trust will have increased the gifting.

Gift giving expresses our essential connectedness to the cosmic process of creation. The vast emptiness continually draws the gift of new being into itself, and creation expands. Everything that is, is a gift. When we treat it as such we simply allow for the continuous movement of increase by which we all come to be more fully. Each of us is a gift, receiving and giving all that we are each moment. I become that in myself which I give as gift to the world. I continue to become for so long as I am able to give myself away. This is the paradox.

In our culture we remain leery of giving ourselves away, and with good reason. For too long we were taken. We made deals in order to survive. We distorted our own deepest understanding of our powerful emptiness and the increasing gift we could become in our worlds. But not to give is not the solution to our dilemma. Possessing whatever we can get, stopping the movement and filling the emptiness, will destroy us.

Instead we must honor the gift. If we can be empty enough, if we can purify the vastness within us enough to perceive clearly, we will not be taken. Nor must we sell ourselves. There are times when we need to refuse a "gift": when bonding is inappropriate, impossible, or could prostitute our souls. There are also times we must not give:

when it is a bribe, when there is no emptiness in the other to call forth the gift. So we must discern. We must reflect.

If you have two coats, Jesus tells us, and you come across a person who has none, give one away. Let the gift move into the emptiness, for that is the nature of gift. So the gift with which Beth always blessed the stranger moved into the emptiness she felt in the troubled girls who came to visit her. And her gift moved into me also. For when I am trusting enough to empty myself, to "clear the stuff from my attic," and to welcome the Stranger within, I *do* hear within me what Beth promised: the music of an ongoing creation, the clear Song of the Holy One—a Gift of Blessing growing in movement and power as it flows through the increasing vastness of my womansoul.

Dancing the New Year In

Blessed are those who mourn,
they shall be comforted.

LOST ON A THRESHOLD

When my mother looks at me her eyes are vacant. The one she calls "the girl at the desk" smiles abstractedly while securing her into the geri-chair.

"She wants to get away," the woman tells me. "She wanders, so she could get lost. Last week she made it past the gates and down the street to the Standard Station. Asked the attendant to take her home, to help her find the way. He called the rest home."

The girl at the desk leaves us alone. I search my mother's eyes. Both of us are lost.

I am a child standing at the edge of the woods. I am quite young—seven, perhaps. For a long time, for as long as memory, I have known the woods conceal a castle of indescribable beauty. Those who dwell there have bodies light as air and voices of music. They live forever. At the castle's center a fountain springs forth from a place with no beginning. The fountain is shaped like a chalice or a breast, and its water is so pure that those who drink of it never die.

On this particular day I have dressed myself in silk scarves, draping them around my body in a fashion that feels both seductive and spiritual. I am naked underneath and the lake breeze deliciously penetrates the violet, red, green, and blue silk. My instinct is toward some meeting, some rendezvous deep in the woods. Just past the first trees a red-orange tiger lily beckons, and beyond that, wild roses.

My mother warned: Don't ever go into the woods. One time an old woman who was staying near here wandered in to pick wildflowers. Each flower looked lovelier than the last and she went deeper until, when she tried to return, she discovered that she was lost. For three days and three nights she wandered, eating only what the woods provided—wild berries, roots. Each day she became a year older. On the fourth morning some fishermen on the lake heard her call. She was standing waist deep in the swamp, her white hair unbraided and tangled around her shoulders, her blue eyes shining with insanity. They took her into the boat and brought her back to land. Her family, grateful for her life, took her from here and they never returned. So don't go into the woods. You could die there.

My mother is dying. But it is because she is lost that we cry. My sister confesses she sometimes wishes our mother *would* die. We sit in the California sun watching a hummingbird sip sweetness from a fuchsia. She runs her finger over the rim of her teacup and I feel her mind absent itself while her mouth says the words, "I feel guilty saying this, but sometimes I wish she would die." The hummingbird seems not to move. We are framed by the words, stopped in the progression of our own lives, a still photo in the album of memory. How much power do wishes have? Will the phone ring now? Will it have happened now that the words have been formed and sent into the universe on waves of air?

"It's all right," I hear myself speaking, "dying is not the worst of our fate. She *wants* to die, you know." My sister cries then. And I think she is crying not only for the mother who is lost, but for the mother she had never found, and now never would. Unless, perhaps, within herself.

We are silent in the sunlight. Dying may not be the worst, but it has always seemed so. The mother cannot die, must not die: This law is fundamental in the heart of each child. That child who lives still within me sees again the images of the dream, the one she has feared since first she could remember.

The first time she had still been in her crib, covers tucked securely around her, an enormous safety pin holding them in place. Somehow the crib's bars, the first thing she saw upon wakening, have become a part of the dream now, and the screaming is part of the dream as well. It is so hard to know in the dark what is dream anymore and what is real and if Mommy is alive or dead in the terrible fire that she cannot stop. A monster machine—an orange road grader with serpentine legs for wheels and with fire shooting out its top—coming down the road, coming, coming—and the driver man laughing— coming toward the white house where Mommy is—it will burn the house down—it will kill Mommy—stop it, Christin, stop the monster machine, don't let it kill Mommy! But it is so big. She wants to stop it. She has to stop it! She can't stop it! She is too little.

"Mommy! Mommy!" the child screams, *"Mommy!"* Then the mother, alive after all, turns on the light, cuddles the small girl, and croons, "It's all right, Christin, Mommy is here, it was only a dream, only a dream."

Do what are only dreams become in time what only is real? I wonder this in mid-life, as I pound on the locked windows of the white house where my mother lies dying. This house is real. It is on Highland Parkway in St. Paul, Minnesota. The early March snowdrifts are piled around it, smoke comes from the chimney, the lights are on, the windows and doors are locked, there is no response to my knocking.

We had plans. She would pick me up, and my sister, and the three of us would drive to the hospital to visit my aunt who had just had surgery. But she is late. I call—no answer. Well, there must have been an errand. Later I call again. Still no answer. Frantic, but not aware yet of being frantic, I drive to the house she has been renting less than a month. Funny, I never saw before how it is like the dream-house. I pound. My mind is suspended, I don't let it think, don't let the realization come. But I drive wildly home for the key— and back. My sister is with me now. We open the door and call. No answer. Tentatively we enter the white house.

Mother is slumped on the bathroom floor. She is breathing but she won't wake up. "Mother, mother, can you hear me?" *(Mommy, I can't save you, I am too little.)* Call 911. I touch her face and whisper, "Wake up now, Mother." *(Don't die, Mommy, don't die.)* Down close to her ear, I can feel her uneven breath. "Oh my God," I whisper, "I am heartily sorry for having offended Thee . . ." My tears fall on the mother's cheeks.

Now she sits lost somewhere between worlds; and I sit half a continent away trying to understand how she got lost in the deep woods of the human soul on her way to death. How can I comfort her? How can I be comforted? We both stand on a threshold, mourning the loss of something we could not even know while we had it.

I open the metal box in which my mother kept her precious things all throughout the years I was a child. I sort through the letters, pictures, and books.

"For the first time in six years I failed to dance the New Year in."

So she spoke to her diary on the first day of 1931. It was the only year she kept a diary. She was twenty, and it was a turning point: the year she fell in love with my father and the year she felt the first signs of tuberculosis. "I am worried about myself," she writes on a rainy November day. "I just had a coughing spell and I spit a lot of blood—must be a reason. I hope it isn't TB. Please don't let it be TB." Before six months had passed she was leaving home for the sanatorium at Ah-Gwah-Ching. I've seen the pictures. She and my father are both dressed in white—stylish, F. Scott Fitzgerald fashion. Her marcelled hair waves down on one side of her forehead under her "flapper" hat. His slicked-back black hair and trim moustache are reminiscent of a young Clark Gable. Both of them are smiling. Both of them knew she might not return. "He was a brave man to have married me," she wrote in her late sixties, after he had died. "Many TB victims didn't survive . . . but we were in love."

The Depression fills her account of the year. Boredom alternates with frenetic activity. Wild dances and Prohibition liquor almost every weekend. Days of waiting in lines of more than one hundred women hoping to be interviewed for a $20-per-week secretarial job. Movies almost every day as a way to break the monotony. *The Birth of a Nation* is the only one she mentions that I recognize. The others must have been immensely forgettable: *The Criminal Code,* with Walter Huston; *The Way of All Men,* with Douglas Fairbanks, Jr.; *Going Wild,* with Joe E. Brown; *Way for a Sailor,* with John Gilbert; *The Lash,* with Richard Barthelmess. And these all in the first week of January. "It was mighty poor entertainment," she comments.

She dreamed of romance, movie style.

I see you, Mother, not my mother yet. You are someone separate whose life has nothing to do with me. I became but a small part of the wholeness of you. I see you before I was, before you thought of me, before you wanted me. You wear silk pajamas, soft coral, and you stand before your art deco mirror pondering yourself. You wonder who you are. Who you resemble. Greta Garbo? No. She was much too self-contained and you burst forth with everything you feel. Barbara Stanwyck? How you wish! For she is George's favorite, especially when she cries her celluloid tears. But your face is too soft, too sentimental. Bette Davis? Never!

Who? How awful to be common!

You shake your head as if to drive away the images and regard more directly those brown doe-eyes of yours. You wonder why, despite all the friends you have, you see so much loneliness there. You turn to the bed, sit cross-legged, and begin to write in your diary. "Nothing's happening tonight. This is a lonesome old evening—but then, I need some sleep so I guess I'll go to bed early." You close the Morocco-leather book and sit a moment more. Then on impulse you wind up your portable phonograph, set the needle down on Wayne King's "The Waltz You Saved For Me," and dance around the room, smiling, and alone.

What is the center of this, the point from which the feeling spirals? The dream could have been it, but it's more a foreshadowing, a seeing on the part of the child. The lonely dancing in the bedroom is another foreshadowing, but this time a seeing on the part of the mother.

We remember so little, really; and what a child sees bears scant relationship to the mother's reality. There are the stories, of course, but how have we edited them to fit our self-understanding? What remains of a life so precious? And what is forever lost?

Yet I am obsessed with this requirement: to save my mother from oblivion. And how shall it be done, since all I know of her is what has become a part of me? And who shall I save in the recording of these things? Because she is *my* mother, which means a part of me cannot live on if she is lost. So is it myself I save in the telling?

You may ask what really happened here and what is fabrication. I must admit that I no longer know—if ever I *did* know. I know the color of her eyes, the way her lips felt soft on my forehead. I know the sound of her voice, for I hear it in my dreams.

Everything happened. Whether waking or in a dream, I no longer know. Doesn't all of the past become a dream, finally? And doesn't the dream reveal the secret?

My mother wanted to be a writer. "Remember these stories," she would say to me, "because someday you must write them down. I so wanted to be a writer, but I guess I never had the time—or perhaps the discipline to stick with it. One thing led to another. There was the Depression, and the tuberculosis, and later working hard with your father just to make ends meet—the resort, the airport, the gift shop—we pulled through. Then, of course, we had you girls to bring up. And now it seems too late."

And now it *is* too late. She can't remember how the typewriter works, and her hand shakes too much to sign her name. What messages she can still send are brief and written by a rest home volunteer: "I enjoy your letters very much. I am happy to hear about your book. At the present time I feel good. I do think of you and pray for you. Much love, Mother."

What are the stories, really? Common events tucked away in memory because they held some secret key to unlock the meaning of a common existence. But was it common to her? Would it be common to me if I could understand? Is the story each of us has to tell so crucial that without it some pattern in the fabric of the world is left incomplete? And what responsibility have I, now, as the repository of her stories—now that she is lost?

MIDWIVES

We are midwives in the between-times: The creation that is the cosmos, and each of us who feel lost on its threshold of becoming, need the midwife's powerful intent to pull us through. We need the midwife who lives in each of our souls to coach the birthing of an ever-new and renewing womanself. We need to be midwife to others, lending our energy to their heroic attempts to break through barriers of the lifeless into new life. Together we need to midwife the world.

The midwife enters the lost places with her who will give birth. The midwife is the woman-between: the liminal woman, the threshold woman. She focuses her energy upon the process of coming through. Coming through birth. Coming through disease. Coming through death. She keeps us breathing, keeps us one with the universal rhythm of creation. She sings the song of breath, turning our fear and the frenetic struggle resulting from it in intricate dance of becoming. "Behold, the Holy One make things new," she reminds. "She dances the New Year in; she dances in your soul; she *is* the dance of your soul bringing you through, making you new."

The loss we experience in the between-times is threefold: loss of identity or name, loss of a sense of our own history or time, and a loss of community or home.

The woman lost between-time no longer can remember her own name. When Alyce, my mother, drifted up from the deep places of coma after her stroke we asked her if she knew who she was. "My name is Rosalind," she smiled.

"Who are these people?" I questioned, showing her a picture of her and my father standing one on each side of me as a child. "Those were your father and mother," she replied.

Pointing at her picture I said as gently as I could, "This is you, Mother. Your name is Alyce." She stared at me tolerantly, uncomprehendingly.

This drastic loss of name stands as a metaphor for a loss that is more subtle but no less real. Any radical change, any passage from one way of being to another, can leave us stranded for a while in the between-time. From single woman to spouse, from career woman to full-time mother, from fertile to menopausal woman, from wife to divorced woman or widow. When I lose my name I no longer have the power to be present in a meaningful way to myself or to others. Every past event through which I discovered the significance of my self seems irrelevant to my present existence. I feel inadequate to the task of life, lost, an anonymous woman on the threshold of being someone again.

Isolation in the present moment with no before or after describes "loss of time." But the present is not static; it is so fleeting as to be constantly lost. The woman between-time can be overcome with fear at this fluidity, at this powerlessness to catch hold of a moment of time or way of being, at this complete lack of security. No longer experiencing time as continuous or consecutive, linking the past and the future, she may feel herself moving at light speed into nothingness or chaos. Her past seems to rise up as meaningless and disconnected from what is now; her future stretches out in a dark uncertain void into which the present moment streaks and disappears. Denial of her past and fear of her future leave her abandoned in a "now" without content. She is lost, between. She could disintegrate there unless she can be pulled through into the New.

Finally, the woman living between-time loses her sense of being at home. Stripped of a significant identity and set adrift in time, she finds herself incapable of relating to others as she has been accustomed. Good friends seem like strangers because they expect her-who-used-to-be. Or they seem like enemies because they are a painful reminder of what has been lost. Places where she no longer feels at home mock her. Those places, invested with meaning by her experience of the past, now stand as silent witnesses to the impossibility of her living any longer that way of life she formerly loved but now has lost. The woman between-time becomes one of the disinherited, the dispossessed—a stranger in a strange land.

The midwife calls us by name, measures time by our breath, and sings of home. When we dance to her song, stepping through the emptiness of the between-space, we arrive, finally, in the promised place. She is the dreamer who envisions what is possible, and we, by believing, give birth to the dream in ourselves.

When Pat, my first spouse, died of cancer in what should have been the middle of his life, a community of women and men were midwife to his passage. Each of us who called to him, touched his body, measured the ebb and flow of his labored breath, sang songs to him throughout the night, had a passage of our own to walk through some kind of death-to-what-we-were into a new being.

The midwife shares the journey of the one who walks between-lives and is herself transformed by the birthing.

A group of twenty women circled Pat and prayed:

> You are in our womb—the womb of womanbody-womansoul.
> We call you forth into life and greet you with a new name.
> Leave behind you the dis-ease, and come forth dancing!
> Majestic Stag drinking cool waters from the River
> of Life, be born and live!
> Great Eagle poised upon the highest peaks of the
> Everlasting Mountain, be born and soar!
> Son of the Great Mother, come forth from the darkness
> of Her vast and pulsing Body: be alive!

Strong and brilliant Rock, survive!
Dreamer of new worlds, dream on!
Man of laughter, tears, and song, we call you forth—
Man of visions and of words, we call you forth—
Man fathering hope in the souls of many, we call you
forth!

Whatever kind of death this birthing requires of you, we offer you our energy, our womanstrength, and the secure space of this womanwomb to give you courage and sustenance for the passage. Remember us when you are born anew.

Then they gave him pure water to drink, a daisy for tenacity, a rose for spirit, and the kiss of peace.

When the labor of his breathing extended into days and nights I held my hand upon his heart and on his lungs, breathing in and out in unison. Whenever his breathing caught and the struggle against suffocation began I whispered, "Peace." The struggle left him and we measured the time in breath once more. What would the New Time be, the Time beyond breath?

The second afternoon of continuous labor Suzanne brought me food and drink. "This is a drink the midwives give to women in labor. It will give you strength to continue." Edith propped my body up with pillows to minimize the stress on muscles pulled wrong by leaning over the hospital bed. P.J. and Suzanne massaged my neck and head. At night Bernadette pleaded, "Go to sleep, now, Christin; I will count the breathing. I will tell the time til Birth." Alla and Phil flew in from Oregon, stayed the night, and sang songs of living.

Birth came the next afternoon. Pat pushed, like a woman in labor. All at once what he had been was empty; he now filled the room, the hospital, the city, and began his journey into the stars. Edith felt him walking beside her as she and Joseph went toward the parking lot. "Pat died," she said. "We have to go back!"

I wonder sometimes, now, what he is named in his new life, what is the nature of his time, and how fathomless his home. Birth of every kind will always remain a mystery.

A SHOWER OF DIAMONDS

I lay beside John in the darkness of our bedroom. We had just said good night in the gentle, reassuring ritual adopted early in our marriage. Usually I am only momentarily aware of his warmth holding me before I fall asleep, but I was caught up in the contradictions confronting me in this story-weaving about loss. I spoke into the night, not really expecting any answer to the mystery.

"What happens to all we've known, all we've loved? What happens to all that is lost, all that dies in the universe?"

Immediately, John's response: "It showers us with diamonds!"

Of course! I laughed with delight and with love, remembering the small article I had recently discovered tucked away in an obscure section of the daily paper. Dying stars send particles into the universe, and from these new worlds are formed. So we are made of star dust. It is in our blood and bones; in the air we breathe, in the rocks and seas and plants. We have known this for a long time, but only recently have we discovered that the dust from dying stars has the chemical composition of diamonds. The death of a star showers us with diamonds.

So much seems lost as we pass from one threshold to the next in our lives. The losses are not always so dramatic nor so large as the death of a spouse or the failure of one's mental powers. But the losses are daily. Your daughter turns fourteen and will no longer share secrets with you. Your dearest friend is not at home when you call in need of her advice. Your wedding ring slips off while you are swimming in the ocean. You break a dish that belonged to your great-grandmother. Your new car gets scratched and dented in the supermarket parking lot. Leaves fall in autumn. A flower dies.

Because of all the outrageous pain in the world—wars, famine, chronic and fatal disease, betrayal and treason, exploitation of the powerless and poor, genocide, the pollution of the earth and air, the threat of nuclear holocaust—we tend to minimize the daily losses. But they affect us, nonetheless. They leave a mark upon our souls in the form of a question to Life itself. If we refuse to admit the power of small losses, we will surely be overwhelmed by those that are great.

I am reminded of the day the city cut down the giant elm tree on the boulevard between my house and the Ellis's, next door. Anna Sophia Ellis was three years old at the time. Dutch elm disease had spread to many of the trees in St. Paul. We had already lost more than ten along our block, ten trees that once had canopied the street and given shade and beauty to our environment. But the giant elm had stayed.

That spring we talked in concerned tones about the length of time our tree took to produce its fresh green leaves, and how long they seemed to take to grow, and then how thin they seemed against the sky. A ghostly white, leafless branch stuck up from the center, high up. We tried to ignore it. The summer passed.

Finally, one October afternoon after work, we found a blood-red ring painted around the tree's trunk, and a sign tacked up: "No parking this block Friday. Tree removal."

Thursday after dark Suzanne and John, Jesse and Anna, Pat and I gathered by the tree. John thanked it for its long life and the shade it gave the children while they played. We circled it then. Gave it a hug.

Everyone stopped what they were doing the next day when the tree removal crew drove up in front of the house. I was seeing a client, an artist with deep feeling for nature. We postponed our session to bear witness to this loss. Suzanne stood between Jesse and Anna on their porch next door.

Jesse jumped when the tree fell; Anna hid her eyes; a nuthatch screamed.

When the crew had hauled away the branches and trunk and all that remained was an enormous raw wooden table where our elm had been, when all the people had returned to their houses and the everyday tasks of their lives, I saw Anna approach the place where the tree had been. First she walked slowly around the new tree-table. Then she climbed up on it. For a moment she stood, seeming in wonder at the loss, or perhaps at her own body being now where only that morning stood such an enormous and majestic creature. Then she raised her little arms to the sky and tiptoed around and around the tree's circles of years. Dancing.

We once set death and life in opposition to each other and ever since have suffered from the mystery that contradiction sets in motion. But death does not eliminate life, it transforms life. The star transforms into a shower of diamonds, which dance a new world in. There is loss. Surely we cannot deny that there is loss. The old form is lost. We feel ourselves for a time un-formed—between forms. Our experience of loss unsettles us, moves us, changes us—it is the process by which we traverse the between-times toward a new name, a new time, a new home.

Although I did not plan it so, I do not believe it mere coincidence that I am writing this chapter during Holy Week, the remembrance of Christian Passover. The times encourage me to seek out the connections between the most essential mystery of Christian faith and the deepest experiences of womansoul. What are the implications here for the living of a WomanChrist spirituality?

We know the story. Shamefully he died; and with him all our hope. We called him dreamer, storyteller, healer of wounds in body and in soul, teacher, lover, lord. We called him failure—nailed to the tree, struggling for breath, telling the time in breath until the world would end. Then we didn't know what to call him who called us friends and asked us to live on in his name. So the world lives between-times until we learn the name of him who died, in whom we live.

The name we thought we knew has been used to oppress us. Because we are women we are said not to be in his likeness.

There has been a terrible mistake.

He failed. He failed to live a divided life. He failed at class and race and sex discrimination. He failed to despise poverty and pain. He failed to raise himself above an earthly life concerned with preparing meals, nursing sick friends, fishing, enjoying flowers and birds, cavorting with untouchables like tax collectors and whores. He failed to use his considerable talents to advance in the established institutions.

He failed at almost everything the world considered important.

Who, then, lives in his Name? Something was lost in his death, or should have been. The old form of the world killed him. If we live in his name we become the transformation of the world. We become the shower of diamonds from the dying ChristStar.

Those who would use his Name to exclude woman, or to discriminate against us, or to regard us as inferior or not complete in all the subtle ways this has been done have never really learned the Name of which they speak. They live still in the old world, the world that died when Jesus died. They live, formed by an illusion not by truth. "I am the Truth," he said. "All that live according to Truth hear my voice."

The truth is that he excluded nothing created. All-that-is comes together in him. Not that it was not connected before—it was, it always was as it proceeded out of the womb of the Holy. But we pulled it apart, tearing creation, rending the garment of God. This part of the garment is good, and this bad; this we accept, this we reject as unclean, defiled, outcast. Nothing is unclean except what comes from an unclean heart.

Light torn from darkness. Men torn from women. The masculine torn from the feminine within the human soul. White skin torn from skin of color. Spirit torn from matter. Reason torn from sensation. Soul torn from body. God torn from Goddess. Yahweh torn from Shekhinah. Jesus torn from Sophia. Christ torn from women.

Because of these divisions, Jesus was killed. That death should have taught us. The lawmakers judged Jesus unclean: He eats with tax collectors and whores. You know a person by the company he keeps.

Peter figured it out on the roof of Joppa. God lowered a gigantic sheet from heaven—in it was everything "unclean." "What you have considered unclean, Peter, comes from heaven! From *heaven*, Peter. Learn the truth. The laws of the Holy One are not the laws of man."

Some women say we need to get beyond Jesus. It is not that he excluded us; but his name has been coopted through the centuries and used to oppress us. In the name of the Christ we have been battered, burned, raped, isolated, excluded, called unclean, locked up in marriages arranged by our fathers, denied education, denied a voice in the community of Christians. We have been taught in the name of

Christ to serve and sacrifice, to be victim and to give away our power. We have been told to carry the cross with Christ and to feel honored at the opportunity.

When I was a small girl my mother and I attended Stations of the Cross each Wednesday during Lent and on Good Friday. I loved the pageantry: a parade of men and boys dressed in flowing robes, carrying candles, crosses, and incense. A dance of the congregation rising and falling to our knees, singing and chanting words. But the most mysterious to me was the phrase I repeated with everyone after every one of the fourteen stations of Jesus' humiliation and death: "With Christ I am nailed to the cross; and I live, now not I, but Christ lives within me."

We were being asked to believe that being on the cross with Jesus, sharing in humiliation, failure, and pain was *good!*

Jesus died on the cross of contradiction. Jesus died of our dualistic thinking and the laws that arise from it. Jesus died because we rent the garment of the Creation of God. Jesus "died once, for all." It is wrong to repeat it.

So far we have, for the most part, failed to carry out his commission to us: "Live on in my name." To live in the name of Christ is to take up his essence, his identity. It is to refuse to live according to laws and ideas that tear at creation. His name has not been honored. Our task, now, is to redeem the name of Christ.

We don't do that by mimicking his actions. Rather, we live in his name and redeem that name by living the truth. All creation comes forth from the womb and the mouth of the Holy One. Nothing is unclean. The task of each of us is to expand the name of Christ. We must live as wholly and as truly in each of our lives as he did in his; and we must make ourselves continually more aware of our oneness with one another, so that by love and compassion we can heal what is torn in creation. We do this by being what we are: women. We do it by birthing, by loving, by taking life to heart. We do it by expanding to the limits of possibility what our lives can be:

Womanlovers, women-making-homes, women-building-cities, womensingers, womenwriters, womenartists, women-wandering-the-world, womenpreachers, womenpoets, womenfarmers, women-builders, women-making-food, women-making-children, women-actors, womenhealers, womendancers, women-in-protest-against-oppression, womenmourners, womenweavers, women-in-business, womenscientists, women-who-gaze-at-stars, women-who-make-ritual, womenpriests, womenspouses, women-leading-nations, women-who-plant-trees, womenfishers, womenquesters, women-who-climb-mountains, womenadventurers, womenthinkers, women-who-live-alone, women-who-care-for-animals, women-who-talk-to-God.

We do not need to get beyond Jesus the Christ; we need to expand his name. We need to live out of his name. We need to refuse to allow his name to be used as an oppression, or as a justification for our victimization. We are the diamonds from his dying Star. We are WomanChrist.

BLESSED ARE THOSE WHO MOURN

It is midnight between Holy Saturday and Easter. A woman, alone in her house, loosens and brushes her long hair; it hasn't been cut in three years. She then steps into the shower and lets cool water wash her body.

"May this water, first of creatures that filled the womb of the Divine Mother from which all comes, cleanse me from all that defiles, all that oppresses, all that diminishes. From water, on this night, may I be born—new."

She steps from the shower, dries herself, and clothes her body in a flowing white gown. The house is dark. The woman knows her way in darkness. On a circular table in the living room rests a large candle swirled with rainbow colors. For a moment she stands silently beside it. She breathes deeply. The scent of almond fills the night.

> "Christ, yesterday and today
> The beginning and the end"

She strikes a match, catching her breath as the tiny flame bursts and seems to fill the room. She lights the candle.

"Lumen Christi
Deo gratias"*

"Mother, within whose womb I have been buried from the beginning of recorded time, give birth to me tonight. Father, whose lightning opens the tomb, bring me forth from the kingdom of death. I stand before You between the times, in the Name and Image of the Christ. I stand before you as woman. WomanChrist. Bring me forth in this Name, bring forth this world, newborn and alive!"

"Exult oh heavens and be glad oh earth
for this is the night
when Christ came forth from death
and heaven was wedded to earth
and earth to heaven."**

The woman lifts the candle and walks out of her house into the clear night. Stars canopy the earth. She lifts the light to the stars and sings three times in an ancient melody that ascends with each repetition like the song of a lark:

"Alleluia. Alleluia. Alleluia."

Then to the music of breath, of blood, of the breeze in the almond trees, of the whirling stars the woman begins to dance. Lifting the light, bowing to the earth, bare feet in the dewy grass—the woman dances the New Year in.

Mourning is the dance of the soul between-time. The measured steps of the women on the way to the tomb. The widow circling the bed of her just-dead spouse; a circle-dance like the moon round the earth casting peace in silver light. Miriam's dance on the shores of

* From the Roman Catholic Liturgy for the Vigil of Easter. Dom Gaspar Lefebure, O.S.B., *St. Andrew Daily Missal* (St. Paul, MN: E. M. Lohmann, 1958), 475.

** Paraphrased from the "Exultet" in the Roman Catholic Liturgy for the Vigil of Easter. Dom Gaspar Lefebure, O.S.B, *St. Andrew Daily Missal* (St. Paul, MN: E. M. Lohmann, 1958), 475.

the sea between two lands. Anna's journey round the rings of age in the giant elm.

The mourning dance begins in courage and brings comfort. "Blessed are those who mourn, they shall be comforted." Mourning moves womansoul in improvised steps toward a new time. The dance of mourning is as active as the dance of birthing. The power of life moves so strongly it seems we cannot but choose to participate. But the new life born from mourning is our own.

The movements of a mourning dance are many, taking a different order in different women's lives or to mark the between-time of different kinds of lostness in the same life.

THE WAILING DANCE

Sound upon the air, it *is* the air, the earth, the sky, everything become sound. Starting deep in tones like gasping for breath, like heartbeat magnified, like earthquakes, like tornadoes coming across wheat fields and over farmhouses and forests. Starting deep—and rising. The bird's scream over the nest empty of eggs now stolen, wail of wolves, cry of banshee, of rabbit out of the terror of the night. Then a keening—long, the melody of whales reverberating through oceans across the world toward the lost one.

Womansoul wailing. World wailing. Out of the void, the depths, the vastness. I hear the cry. I am the cry. I am become sound, a dance of sound, a wailing dance. I am breath dancing in gasps and cries and screams—dancing in an infinity of keening: "Ah" and "Ai-ee" and "Ooohah." Nothing remains of me but the sound. I am only woman-who-wails. I am dissolved in sound.

DANCE OF TEARS

I am filled with tears. Sometimes bitter, tears sting my eyes. Sometimes pure, they cleanse. I cannot but weep. The reservoir of tears never empties but increases as I cry.

In this dance of tears I lift memory in a liquid box. At each circle of the dance an image appears of what was, of what might have been, of what is lost. Through the clarity of tears I learn that what is lost in death is not the past but the might-have-been. I flow on the

tide of tears from what is no more to what will be. The world is
awash; the nightstars blur; at noonday rainbows circle the sun.

STILLDANCE

Pause. No sound. The moment between breath lasting not less than
forever. Arrested. Captured mid-movement. On tiptoe. Arms
stretched out. Hands open. Supplicating the silence. Poised between
lost and waiting. I have suffered an excess of change. My house
gives boundaries to the world; I cannot move from my room. It is not
safe. The empty stillness will explode my soul. I need walls. Close.
The tomb. The womb.

FLIGHTDANCE

I am electric. I pound with the beat of drums through the primitive
night. I race the gazelle. I unbind my hair to the wind. I am wild. I
want release. I throw off my clothes and dance under the moon—my
breasts flow with the juice of life—my belly reflects moonglow. I *am*
the moon. Changing. Moving. Dancing the seasons in. Passion is my
name. I run up hills. I drive fast. I make love with abandon. Like a
star I explode. I rush to the edges of space, to the ends of time. I
break through.

DANCE OF ENDURANCE

I have danced for two years. The steps are all familiar now. So far I
have failed to dance the New Year in. The dancing has become my
occupation. I am a professional. The music now is as common as the
breeze, as rain, as surf. I am empty of tears. I eat because I must. I
let the sunrise wake me from sleep. I exercise to keep my body from
numbness. It could be that I will dance thus all my life; no one can
tell me; no one knows except for herself. I live each moment. I am
tenacious. I will not stop dancing.

DANCE OF COMFORT

The dance is forever. The dancing is the new year; the dancing is the
comfort. The dancer is the dance.

GOD IS A DANCING MIDWIFE

The cosmos is a birthing dance. The dance itself brings forth the music that creation is. For the cosmos is not a "thing" so much as a fluidity of substantial sound, a harmonious dance. In this dance everything pulses with a rhythm of coming to be. At each moment, particularly when we feel ourselves between-times mourning, we participate in the creative process by joining the birthing dance.

A friend who grew up in Saudi Arabia tells me that when a woman there begins her labor, she is surrounded by a circle of dancing midwives. For the duration of her birthing the women take turns dancing the birthing dance. It is a powerful, undulating, sensual participation in the dance of birth itself. The music draws its rhythm from the contractions of the womb, from the pulsating of the universe. The dancing midwives with the laboring mother at their center becomes more than themselves alone; they are one with the dance of birth. They are a microcosm of cosmogenesis. They are the birthing. They are the dance.

It is not only in our individual lives that we are between-time. We suffer not only the loss of our personal names and homes. We are mourners in a between-time world, a civilization that has lost its name. We are gathered at a moment when labor is beginning and are asked to be midwives to a new culture, to participate in a dance that circles the globe.

Dance is our spirituality. The dance in the womb where opposites are joined to become a new creature. The dance of the stars that explode, showering diamonds that coalesce to form new worlds. The dance of visions and dreams out of which our future is made. The dance of love, which perceives connections and unites what has been separated.

"How does God keep track of it all?" Pat wondered often. In a plane over New York City: "Just look at all of those buildings, filled with people loving and learning and working and playing and hoping for everything in their lives. And God is supposed to know them all by name, and to have counted each hair on each of their heads! How does God do it?" Driving through the wheat fields of the Red River Valley: "Does God keep track of each stalk of wheat, each cricket singing that prairie song we hear, each meadowlark, each sapphire dragonfly? Surely God can't. God must just form the broad strokes of the plan of creation and leave the particulars up to us. Or maybe it's angels that keep track of the minutiae."

Maybe it *is* angels. He was teasing, of course, to build the wonder, to emphasize the marvelous beauty and the unspeakable vastness. But one day after he died I stood gazing at the spring-green California hills, and the question was posed again out of the clear reservoir of memory: "How does God keep track of it all?" Immediately everything that gave me the illusion of distinctness from the hills, the breeze, the sky, the ground on which I stood disolved. There were no minutiae. There was only one being, and it wasn't me. All of creation, the entire cosmos, including me, was one living organism; and the soul of the organism, the life by which it continued to expand and birth itself, was Love.

This experience was timeless. I don't know how long it lasted, because while it was happening to me I simply didn't *know* anything. It was only when it was over, and I felt myself someone separate again, that I had the sense of having learned something. God doesn't need to keep track because God *is* the living core and source of All; and All is One. And the One is Dancing Love.

We are between-times. In our old experience each of us was a subject and everything else in the universe was an object, "other" from us. We also formed "subject groups" and every other group was objectified. Most often the "center" of life and truth was experienced to be coextensive with the "subject." The "objective other" was off center, eccentric, often wrong, sometimes evil. This experience brought us tribes and nations and other offshoots: competition for survival, national and racial and religious discrimination, and war. The experience also encouraged sexism, slavery, economic subjugation, and the exploitation of natural resources. Whatever the object might be, it could be "used" to enhance the "subject."

In our new experience we are beginning to realize that the object does not exist. Everything is connected, is one. What I do to anything or anyone affects the whole organism of which I am part, and therefore affects me. Whatever I bring to birth into the universe becomes, immediately, a facet of my own being and the being of everything.

Everything is a part of the dance. In order to dance this new world in we need a spirituality of attention, intention, and consent. Attend to the center, which is everywhere. Listen for the music rising from the heart of the cosmos, from the essence of Love. Intend to be always a part of the rhythm and the sound. Wherever there is discord modulate half a step to harmony. Consent to the cosmic dance by releasing self-centered control. Join your rhythm to the pulsing of the stars. In the center everywhere the Divine Woman gives birth. We are what is born. We dance around her. She dances within. There is one birth. There is one dance.

I sat looking into my mother's eyes. She lay on the nursing home bed, totally relaxed. During our long afternoon visit I had tried to enter *her* reality—that place in which she seemed lost. I finally gave up words—we couldn't meet there anymore—and touched her face as gently as I could, smoothing back her hair, kissing her forehead, eyelids, petal-soft cheeks.

It isn't so bad, I thought, as I drifted deeper and deeper into those eyes that no longer seemed empty, but infinitely calm. My hand rested on hers, caressing her tenderly. She raised her other hand to my hair and with a touch softer than breeze touched me—my hair, my lips, and down my arm. Her face became love.

Mama, Mama. Perhaps there is no lost place after all. Or perhaps it's where we dare not go because it is too whole. Do you see the castle in the woods? Do you drink the water flowing pure from the breast-shaped cup? Have you discovered where the wildflowers grow?

Mama, your eyes are doors into forever. You are so very near. We have no need of thought, for we are one. Love is your dance. Mama, you have danced the New Year in.

Primal Sacrament

Blessed are the meek,
they shall inherit the earth.

GLORIFY GOD IN YOUR BODY*

The woman stood regally in the center of the WomenChurch circle. She wore vestments: a deep violet-and-rose print sarong wrapped so that it knotted just under her navel, a white sash tied around her breasts, a large colorful beaded yoke around her neck and over her shoulders. Her feet were bare, her skin was dark bronze.

"I will dance the vulva dance for you. But first, let me talk about it a bit.

"As a midwife I am made aware daily of the shame women feel about their genitals. Each time a woman lies on the examining table and spreads her legs her pain is obvious. It's not just the discomfort of the position, or of the instruments used for the examination, it is the exposure of what most of us consider ugly, dirty, smelly, and even evil.

"It has not always been so.

"There was a time when the woman's vagina was venerated as not only something of beauty, but of divinity. Statues were created to honor this gateway through which each person enters into life. In fact, in the deepest parts of ourselves we all know the sacredness of the vagina. There have even been times when women's exposure of their genitals has averted war. Both in Nigeria and in Ireland it is written that when the men had prepared for war and the invading army appeared at the city gates, the women went out and 'lifted their skirts,' and the invaders turned and returned to their cities and war was averted. The vagina, through which all life comes, is the most profound antiwar symbol we possess.

"As I dance, remember the beauty and sacredness of your womanbody. And remember that no matter how your personal body is shaped, whether it is abundant or slight, somewhere in the world a goddess is venerated who looks just like you.

"The dance is in three parts."

---

* 1 Corinthians 6:20 NAB

She turned, removed the sash from her breasts, and placed a long white lace veil over her head and face; then she turned again to face us. The music began. Subtle. Drumming. Human voices delicate as birds. Wordless. Her body began to undulate. Her belly pulsed in and out. Her pelvis rocked. Over and over her hands formed a triangle, speaking to us in signs of the holiness of the vulva. Her flowing garments both hid and revealed her womanness. The dance spoke:

I am woman. I am sacred. I am the body of life, of birth, of pleasure. Although I am hidden, remember how beautiful I am. From my breasts pours the milk of sweetness. Through my vagina comes new life. I thrust. I take in. I give forth. I am strong and I am holy.

When she had completed the first part of the dance she took the lace veil from her head and tied it onto the yoke so that it hung over her pubic arch. She then removed the sarong so that she was naked except for the veil, which concealed and revealed. Her face as she danced seemed the face of a Goddess, proud and powerful.

When the entire ritual of the dance had been once again completed, she removed even the sash, so that she stood before us wearing only the beaded yoke. Again the dance began. Nothing now could hide the wonder and strength of womanbody. Nothing could restrain the exaltation of this gateway to life. The music pulsed on. The dance continued. Over and over she used her hands to give the sign of the vulva, of the flowing breasts, of the labor of birth, of the majesty of woman.

The music stopped. She stood for a moment, then reached for her robe. WomenChurch applauded. WomenChurch rose to its feet, and applauded in overflowing gratitude. Dancing before us, this woman became a womanpriest. She redeemed us from our shame. She proclaimed our beauty with her body.

The woman next to me, a nun, whispered, "That was so beautiful I wish I could go now to be by myself to savor it." I was thinking, I wish I could go now to be with John so we could savor this womanbody of mine together. Whether we women are sexually celibate or sexually expressive lovers our bodies are exquisitely sensual and sacred.

But the deep-bronze priestess was right. We were not taught to love our bodies. When we read in Scripture that we were to glorify God in our bodies, many of us concluded that we were to transform our bodies into a spiritual entity—such as we assumed God to be. It never occurred to most of us that our bodies might actually be *revealing* God, so that the more aware of and loving toward our bodies we became, the more glory we gave to God.

As I write I am painfully aware of the comparative ease I felt reflecting on a spirituality that rises from the experience of loss or death to what I feel now, reflecting on sexuality. What kind of body-memory do I have that transforms death but imprisons this power of sex in a net of resistances, denial, restrictions, and—I hesitate to name it because I so want it to be gone—shame? I search my spiritual tradition. Some explanation resides there, certainly.

The revelation of Yahweh to the Hebrew people dawned in reaction to the Goddess religion, which abounded in the Mediterranean area. This Yahweh became understood by the people as a warrior god leading Israel on a linear path toward a future unbounded by the cyclical "eternal return" of the neighboring Goddess cultures. The birth-giving Goddesses, along with the sensuous sexuality they encouraged, were condemned, their altars torn down, their rituals abolished.

Jesus, as he is represented in the New Testament by second- and third-century members of the Christian communities, has little to say about sex. He dismisses sexual "sin" in order to emphasize justice, compassion, love, and the dangers of hypocrisy. We can surmise by his life story that he was probably a somewhat earthy man who loved nature with poetic spontaneity.

We have theologized about his nature as "God" and his nature as "Man." We talk about Incarnational spirituality. From his Incarnation we can assume that the God in him loved bodiliness. So God must also love our bodiliness. Nevertheless we have continued throughout the centuries to distrust our bodiliness, particularly as it is sexual. We have overwhelmed ourselves with catalogs of sexual transgression. We seem obsessed, like Paul of Tarsus, desiring to "be delivered from this body of sin."

We continue to fear the Goddess who, we instinctively sense, could imprison us in matter, could reduce us to instinct, could make us so identical with earth that we could never again rise above it like flame, like air, like a spirit bird climbing, climbing toward the light.

But in our bodies are our wings.

A woman, whom I will call Cara, had cried all day. Now, at twilight, she stands exhausted, bereft of understanding, wrung out with guilt, nauseated with pleading.

"God, why?
Failure fills me to the brim;
It chokes and suffocates me;
Yet I cannot spit it out.
My marriage has failed;
Divorce divides us,
Separates me from my hopes,
Rips out my trust in life.
And you do not deliver me.
You do not forgive.
You leave me torn.
Why?"

Cara waits. The only response is a deepening twilight. She is past thought. Instinctively, ritualistically, she begins to remove her clothes: the small silver bird in flight that hangs around her neck she places carefully in an ebony box; her sandals, light-green summer dress, panties, bra. Each article she folds carefully and places on the bed. Finally, almost naked now, she removes her gold wedding band, holds it pensively for a moment in the fading light, then drops it on the floor. When she hears the nearly imperceptible sound it makes as it hits, she begins to cry again.

In silence Cara walks to the bathroom and fills the tub with warm water. Gratefully she lowers herself into the soothing bath. At first she lies still. The water holds her, warms her, welcomes her. She closes her eyes.

Thoughts have gone completely now. Sensation awakens slowly, deliciously. Cara is wholly embodied, wholly touched by the cleansing, life-giving water. She moves slightly. Water swirls around her like finest liquid silk. Tantalizing. Arousing.

For a moment Cara feels surprise at the subtle beginnings of sexual pleasure. Then she surrenders to the body's wisdom. She moves the washcloth gently over her body, thrilling, increasing sensation. Arms, legs, belly, breasts, thighs, soft folds of labia, rose-petal vulva, become heavy and pulse. She breaths deeply until the breath reaches her swollen inner core. Consciousness lifts on her breath and is suspended. Something releases in her mind, some fist of resistance to herself, and she senses herself rushing into a wholeness as if she were wind whirling with itself. She is beauty. She is cosmic. She is ecstatic. She is a waterfall.

Cara weeps with joy. Some miracle of embodiedness has returned her to herself, forgiven.

She glorifies God in her body, which has become this day a sacrament of new life.

PRIMAL SACRAMENT

Body is the primal sacrament. Through our bodies the Mystery of All is revealed to us. In sexual lovemaking our bodies become expressions of the essence of Life, making us aware of Life's presence and increasing that presence through an intensity of pleasure.

The argument over whether sex is primarily unitive or procreative or equally both seems profoundly limited when we experience sex sacramentally. As a sacrament sex not only intensifies many facets of life, but also communicates the blessing of God. Its symbolism and power are multidimensional.

Sex is sacramental of self-discovery.

Sex is sacramental of intimacy and love.

Sex is sacramental of the union of opposites.

Sex is sacramental of pleasure in creation and of creation itself.

Sex is sacramental of trust, unself-consciousness, and surrender.

Sex is sacramental of atonement and of forgiveness.

Sex is sacramental of promise and commitment.

Sex is sacramental of connectedness in creation and of creation with the Mystery of All.

As sacrament—or embodiment of the graciousness of God, which intensifies as we continue to receive—sex is perhaps the most powerful experience possible. Because sex, as this communicator of the Sacred, is so multivalenced, we can feel overwhelmed as it awakens. The Sacred strikes awesome fear and trembling fascination in us. We feel caught between the instinct to escape the terror and to dissolve into the pleasure of the Holy Presence.

So, over the centuries, we have attempted to desecrate sex in order to be able to bear it.

We desecrate woman's body so it will not reveal the being and power of God.

We desecrate pleasure to control the grace of ecstasy.

We desecrate sexual intercourse and let it fall into banality, tawdriness, mechanical manipulations, and violence.

We have thus lied to ourselves about the presence and the power of God in our bodies, about the responsibility we have for revealing that presence, about the beauty and bliss we embody. Our power of sex turns against us when we forget or refuse to remember our incarnational reality: that we embody the Holy One. When we separate the power of sex from the power of God, the expression of sex from the expression of love, then our very bodies become a sacrilege. WomanChrist spirituality unlocks the power of God in sex by restoring the sacred nature of the primal sacrament.

SELF-DISCOVERY

The girl is thirteen. It is a Saturday morning in summer. She wakes suddenly, early, the sun is just rising. Careful not to disturb the household, she tiptoes down the stairs and through the living room to the front door. Something calls. Something within. Something that must be found in the dawn.

Her bare feet sink into the cushion of dewy grass. The morning air is golden. The girl runs; she runs as if she is flying—without effort, with grace—not like a child but like a woman wrapped in wind. At the top of the rise she lifts her nightgown over her head and unfurling it like a flag she twirls round and round, laughing. She sinks to the grass, alone with the morning.

Dew washes her young breasts. Dew tickles her feet, her legs, and between her legs. She reaches for a dandelion, plucks it, holds it under her chin, and says to no one, "Aha, I *do* like butter!" Then she traces its puff of yellow down her throat and in a figure eight over her breasts until they point with pride and satisfaction at the sky. Down wisps the dandelion, circling her navel, then catching again and again in the new, the soft, the mysterious hair between her legs.

Quiet, satisfied, the girl rests on the earth until the sun dries her dewy body. Then she slips her gown over her head and walks back to the still-sleeping household. A meadowlark sings. She pauses, smiles, and says, "Good morning."

Why, when what we feel is so deliciously earthy, do we often dissociate that feeling from the spiritual? From where comes the sensation that the power of creation needs to be separate from the power of the Creator? The deepest, most intense, most thoroughly bodily pleasure has the power to expand the boundaries of the individual to include the universal pleasure that we name God.

Many of us feel that we should be suspicious of such ecstasy. What if such bliss were to absorb us so completely in creation that we would forget the Creator? Impossible! The whole point of ecstasy and union with the Holy One is the surrender of egocentric control so that God contains us, God creates us, God explodes in pleasure within and around us.

It is not necessary to always be keeping track of God. We can simply *live*. And the Holy Creator of our life delights in the joy of our being. In bodily pleasure the Holy One graces us with the wonder of who and what we are.

The woman dreamed:

I am deep in the woods searching for the hunter who is all wise and possessor of knowledge by which the Holy Bear can be found. I am compelled to search. I come upon a stream alongside of which two women sit drying their long hair in the sun and warm breeze. They belong to a secret sisterhood— priestesses of the Bear. As we talk a silver bell rings in the distance. They rise quickly, saying that the hunter calls.

I follow them along the stream to where it widens into a large river. On an island in the center of the river is a temple of nature. At first I think it is covered with ancient trees, but then I realize that the towers rising to the sky are mysterious structures such as those at Stonehenge. The sisters motion to me to follow, and we swim to the island.

A ritual has begun. Each of the sisters in this nature temple needs to be initiated. One by one they plunge into a crystal cavern, a vaginal tunnel filled with razor-sharp rocks and whirling water. I fear I will be pierced and drown. The high priestess assures me that I will live, but I must brave the cavern. I descend.

No sooner have I entered the water of the cavern than it opens out into a wide sky. I am floating in the air. The hunter welcomes me and leads me to the Bear.

The Bear is larger than the sky. The Bear is everything. The Bear compels, attracts, devastates, will consume me; I want consummation. Tantalizing energies begin to rise within me; my body pulses with desire; my body is moist with newness. I want only to be joined to this marvelous being. I go toward her. I open myself. As I experience her embrace and the accompanying ecstasy I cry out, "Who are you?"

I hear the words as if from the totality of the universe: "Self."

I awaken. My body is dissolving in orgasm. I am weeping. I have never been so happy.

While the awakening of sexuality certainly does not encompass all of self-discovery, it does often serve as a powerfully moving manifestation of a coalescence of energies awakening throughout womansoul. Merely physical sensations do not have the power of primal sacrament that results from a coincidence of all dimensions of being: body-soul-spirit, sense-emotion-mind. One's total being is then open to becoming incarnate of God.

A sexual manifestation of this kind can be so ecstatic as to be transcendent. We can experience union, within ourselves, between ourselves and nature, and of all creation with the divine Mystery-of-All, the being we name God. But if we have a dualistic worldview we will be left confused. Our minds, wanting to separate body from spirit and creation from the Creator, will be tempted to conclude either that sex did not belong with this experience and must be exorcised from it, or that sex actually *is* God. Idolatry, both.

Our beings are the outpouring of life from the mystery of the Godhead. Our sexuality is a manifestation of that outpouring and that mystery; not identical with God, but sacramental of God.

"You know, surely," pleads Paul, hardly realizing the wonder of which he speaks, "that your bodies are members making up the body of Christ; . . . the temple of the Holy Spirit, who is in you?" (1 Cor. 6:15, 19).

Spirituality requires becoming more and more a sacrament of God, truer to the revelation of joy and pleasure opening in our body-souls, more respectful of our sexual being. In this way we receive sexual power and pleasure as a gift of life itself and do not seek to control sexual gratification or manipulate it toward egocentric ends.

INTIMACY AND LOVE

My spouse's eyes meet mine in one of our many ways of making love.

"I know you. I have loved you forever; before you came to me, before I reached out with breath to draw you in, before touch. Before I met you, I knew you. Before I loved myself, I loved you."

He traces the outline of my lips with his finger and cups my face in his large, fine hands. He looks long into my eyes. "I love you; I have loved you; I will love you, forever." Lightly, his lips touch each of my eyelids in a kiss more delicate than petals of roses.

The sacrament deepens and expands as more is revealed and entrusted. The more intimacy we allow, the fuller is the love we "make." If I have permitted my lover to see every facet of myself— the strong and beautiful along with the frail and rejected—his look will be sacramental of that seeing. His look will stimulate energy in every facet of me, enlivening the beautiful, healing the wounded, strengthening the fragile. His touch, his kiss will transform what is untouchable and make it into the held and the received.

This is how love is made: We make love out of each other, together revealing, entrusting, receiving, flowing in and out of each other in an intercourse whose vibrations can be felt into the stars.

Our intercourse sacramentalizes the connectedness of All-That-Is. We allow in our bodies the most mysterious and truest reality: that God is love and everything that loves is an outpouring of God.

In the primal sacrament this is how God comes: In the touch of flesh on flesh, in the passionate fire the Holy One flames forth. Our bodies become our souls' prayer.

O Holy Love,
Infinite Yearning of the universe,
Intense Passion for life,
Pulsing Spiral of creation,
Nothing is without your power.
Within your boundless body
The entire cosmos makes love.
Come to us today
And in the universe of self
   Make Love.
In the quickening of our bodies with the passion of our
souls,
   Make Love.
In the touch of wind,
   Make Love.
In enchanting waves of music,
   Make Love.
In the warmth of morning sunlight,
   Make Love.
In the kiss of lips,
   Make Love.
In the intercourse of eyes,
   Make Love.
In the intoxication of the erotic,
   Make Love.
In the most delicate touch,
In the gentlest breath,
In the most common gifts
Of food, of the body's warmth, of holding tenderly,
   Make universal Love.
You, who have given all,
You, who ask for nothing other than surrender to your
gift,
You, who enter our bodysouls like lightning,
Make Love out of us,
And we will fling it into the stars
For the increase of Your Blessed Glory.

UNION OF OPPOSITES

The woman dreamed:

I am in my basement in the midst of a ritualistic community of women and men. The old Native American woman chants. A whirling begins inside me, a darkness descends, I am transported to a vast plain where I witness a mysterious ceremony.

From each of the four directions comes a magnificent and powerful bull garbed in ceremonial robes. Stately, slowly, deliberately the bulls move into the center of a circle of men where they will be sacrificed.

I have been brought here by the old woman, who weaves while she watches the ceremony of the bulls. She tells me I must remember what I have seen.

When I awaken from the vision, the old woman is still chanting. She asks me to tell what I have seen. The circle of men and women listen. Then the old woman takes a knife made of stone. She approaches a man with long black hair and cuts two slashes in his thumb. He is sitting directly opposite me in the circle. I am vividly aware of him and of the blood that now stains his clothes and contrasts brilliantly with his darkness.

The old woman approaches me. She takes hold of my thumb. I close my eyes and go into a kind of trance as she cuts. The incision feels more painful than anything I have ever known, and with the second cut my body flinches and I cry out. A man in the circle behind me tells me that I must be quiet. I open my eyes in rage. I stand, move to the man who wanted to silence me, and scream: "Are you the one who told me to be quiet?" He admits that he is. I scream, "You have no right to do that! I will do as my body wishes! There are no rules here. This is my ceremony."

Although I screamed, I could barely hear my voice, still being in a trance. I look in awe at my blood-covered thumb. Instinctively I know it is time to mingle my blood with that of the man with the long black hair. I must do this because we are somehow reenacting the ceremony of bulls.

A woman in the circle calls out to me that my vision was sexist because only men were involved in the ceremony of bulls. I tell her that the vision represents the uniting of my feminine with my masculine powers. I am very assertive with her, and very certain of my truth and what I must do next.

I have waited too long. There have been too many interruptions from the circle. The blood on my thumb is drying. An old man takes my thumb in his mouth and sucks on it gently until the blood flows again. Then I creep toward the man with the long black hair. We both crawl across the circle to the center. When we meet we join our bleeding thumbs and mingle our blood. The old woman with the knife watches, satisfied. It is good. Complete.

I am woman. I am a continuum of feminine and masculine energies, both of which need acceptance, each of which completes the other. The man I love is also a continuum of masculine and feminine energies, both of which need acceptance, each of which completes the other. In our sexual lovemaking we embody this union. When our bodies join we become a sacrament of the union of opposites.

Every act of making love can be a healing of the dualistic split. Every joining can serve to mend the tear in the fabric of creation. Sex is redemptive.

But we must accept each other as "opposite" if the joining is to sacramentalize such union, and redeem the sundered human world. Such redemption begins with the sundered self.

In me is something "opposite." I hide it. I fear it. I deny it. I am in awe of it. I desire it. I seek it. I run from it. It is a god. It is a demon. It is strong. It is weak. It cries out like thunder. It bleats. It crushes. It empowers. It is all that I am not. It is in everything I am.

I lie in bed with the sheet pulled over my breasts, waiting. The man I love comes into the room. He is naked. He is beautiful. His strong, angular body moves with deliberate and sensuous grace. Every muscle is alert. His broad chest invites me to rest against him. His legs rise like the tall, straight trunks of trees. But he is unselfconscious. He smiles. His consciousness is turned toward me, his opposite.

We look on each other. Love dissolves fear. We willingly embody what is "other." We agree with our bodies that separations can be overcome, the strange accepted, the most keenly carved divisions reconciled. Everything is one. God is revealed in the union of opposites. The ritual in which we are about to engage is one of mingling: the spirit and the blood, the human and divine.

We join. We enact the sacrament. The Old Woman with the knife watches, satisfied. It is good. Complete.

PLEASURE IN CREATION

I have never borne a child. Now that I am past my childbearing years I mourn this decision, which I made as a very young woman. I would like to have experienced that physical conception, containment, and birthing, which is the ultimate embodiment of all creative acts.

I have given birth. Birthing a transformed self. Birthing new life in a friend, in a client, in her who first gave birth to me. Birthing ideas in words; birthing beauty in all the little corners of my world; birthing wonder in a garden or the child next door.

When I was a young woman in a convent set in a midwestern prairie of shimmering wheat and barley, I had a friend named Julia. Art was her birthing and her pleasure. Julia drew all the children her virginal body would never contain. She found them somewhere within herself in a vast creative womb and let them out by means of colored pencil on a white page. They played and laughed, wondered and wept. She drew her spouse, a Christman emerging from violet shadows. On that face Julia worked long and with the intensity of lovemaking. She penetrated the paper with her gaze and outlined in color what she saw until he finally gazed back at her in an intercourse of eyes.

All creation is erotic. All true pleasure is creative. In Greek mythology Pleasure is the child born of the union of Eros and Psyche, the soul. Yearning or desire begins everything. The most minute particles of being yearn for union, and in the pleasure of coming together create something new. Yearning forms worlds and galaxies. Cells join. People are born. Without the pleasure of this yearning nothing is nor can it be. The pleasure of love may be the most real of anything in the universe.

Sex without pleasure violates those who engage in it and

desecrate its inherent creative power. Dutiful sex violates. Treating sex as the "marriage debt" violates. Sex is sacramental of all creation—of the essential attraction within being out of which newness comes. Sex is sacramental of the attraction of God for and within matter, of God yearning for increased incarnation.

Incarnational spirituality requires a kind of "discipline" of sensitivity to pleasure. A disciple is one who listens. A discipline is a listening. Increasingly, a spirituality deepens, bodysoul becomes alert to the most delicate vibrations of pleasure and yearning.

When my friend Ray returned from the edge of death following heart bypass surgery that almost failed, he had changed. He was overcome with the beauty of the world. The winter limbs of trees against a pearl sky were, in his eyes, "naked ladies, dancing." Everything gave Ray pleasure: the morning light on the river; soft, new needles of pine; a butterfly floating on the breeze; a rose budding, blowing full, falling; the pink flush of warmth on a child's cheek; the curve of a woman's ankle; the trace of a smile; distant laughter. He touched whatever he could. He praised beauty wherever it occurred, which seemed to him everywhere.

For the two years he lived following his surgery he spent a lot of time volunteering at a hospice. There he created life in dying people by sharing their beauty with them, by helping them remember and take pleasure in all the beauty of their lives, by his obvious pleasure in being with them, touching them, singing to them, talking to them, encouraging them to share their beauty with others in the hospice who also shared their fate.

Just a few months ago I read about the "dangers of sexual pleasure" in a church document. I recalled that when I was young I was initiated into the esoteric knowledge of those very "dangers"—primarily of sexual pleasure, but also of the pleasures of the body in any form: the delicious comfort of relaxing in a soft chair, the tantalizing scent of flowers, lotions, and perfumes, the taste of good food. Certain pleasures were permitted; but according to the dualistic rending of our nature, they were pleasures of the mind acquiring spiritual knowledge, and pleasures of the spirit advancing in "perfection." Eventually (and contradictorily) the greatest pleasure in God was said to be an *unfelt* pleasure following the various "dark nights" of the senses, the intellect, and the soul.

Certainly we have periods of no-pleasure in our lives—periods of emptiness and mourning. But it is masochistic to *seek* such loss. And throughout the experience, when it comes, we need to be like Ray— listening for the return of pleasure in everything.

WomanChrist spirituality is incarnational. It encourages us to become vibrantly alive. This aliveness includes a beautiful and plea- surable sexual life. For our sexual expression to be sacramental we must be always open to that pleasurable yearning, which—by its very nature—creates. We make love and expand the boundaries of the universe. Sex that does not do this is not sacramental nor is it worthy of us.

BLESSED ARE THE MEEK

Sex is sacramental of connectedness in creation and of creation with the Mystery of All. The meek inherit the earth because they experience that vital connection, they believe in it; they honor their createdness and commonality with creation.

My teachers always connected purity of spirit with sexual life. If we were pure in spirit, they hoped, we would also be "pure" in body, not sin sexually, and consequently "see God." The Beatitude about the meek inheriting the earth always seemed confusing to my teachers. Meekness, seen as the opposite of domination and assertion, was in the long run supposed to make Christians the rulers of the earth. It was paradoxical, they said, therefore difficult to grasp.

Even as children we saw pretty clearly that "meek" adults inherited very little of anything. "Meek" children were ridiculed or ignored by their peers, taken for granted by adults, and designated "teachers pet" in school. We were told that Jesus was ridiculed and seemed to fail in his life, but in the end he—by being as meek as a lamb before the shearer—inherited the earth. It was hard to understand, so we mostly "took it on faith."

Perhaps if we were to stop associating inheritance with the right to dominate or rule we would understand this Beatitude better. Our interpretations have been confused by dualistic thinking. We interpret as though we could be separated from earth, set above it, become its master. We interpret as though earth were a *thing*, to be manipulated by us, rather than realizing that earth is the larger boundary of our own being. Domination by the "meek" is really no different nor better than domination by the shrewd and crafty. Domination is hubris in either case.

The meek inherit the earth because they recognize and act in accord with their oneness with earth. Their inheritance is to share in the power of earth itself, a power that is elemental, natural, radical, basic to all of life. Theirs is a power with, not over, and they are conscious of this power as it flows through them and becomes creative in their lives.

To be meek is to be permeable, to sense the flow of cosmic creation through oneself, to know one's profound connection to the universe, and to be aware that the energy that flows through each of us is the same as the energy manifesting itself in the intricate song of the nightingale, the swell of the tides, the erupting of mountains, the splitting of seeds that release April's green. The meek experience themselves as they are: natural, one body and one spirit with cosmic being. The meek inherit the earth because they *are* the earth.

Sex is sacramental of this inheritance of the meek. In the sexual experience the power of oneness with earth is given primal expression. In the sexual experience people are conscious in their own bodysouls of the basic attractions by which the creation of the cosmos continues. In the sexual experience people surrender domination over both self and the other to become the pulsing, shimmering, erupting, receiving, orgasmic, creating earth. In making love the meek inherit the earth. And earth is expanded by love.

WomanChrist inherits the earth. WomanChrist joins into one what has been separated by generations of dualism. Those who practice the WomanChrist spirituality of reconciliation will sometimes be called heretic Christians because of their resolve to bring the feminine creative energies into balance with the masculine, to lift the theology of Incarnation into equality with the theology of Redemption.

Occasionally we women— forming our spirituality from the conjunction of our faith experience with our religious beliefs—simply happen upon such a balance, unaware that it makes us "heretical" according to patriarchal church dogmatism. Early in my ministry of spiritual guidance with women I was invited to lecture at a local Christian college. The class concerned women in ministry. My task was to share how I, as a woman, reconciled my sexuality with my Christian theology.

I told my story: the childhood beginnings of spirituality in the beauty of nature, which spoke the language of the Holy; initiation into the ancient, sensuous rituals of the Roman Catholic church, which were rooted in nature, its seasons, its elements of air, water, fire, and earth; the mystical environment of convent, its community of women, its spiritually erotic relationship with the incarnate Christ; theological education in liturgy, with its emphasis on the senses, on play, on the sacramentality of creation; ministry to children by means of embodied care and theology in story; finally the flowering and fruition of each of these experiences of the Holy One incarnate in the Christ through a ministry to women. I hoped, by an emphasis on Incarnation, to assist women in reconciling their sexuality with their Christianity.

"But how is all of that *Christian*?" the professor queried.

"Pardon me?" I asked, somewhat stunned.

"How is it all Christian? You have talked of nature, and ritual, and women, and something about *love* of Christ. But you have said nothing of the essential Christian truths."

Now I was really confused. The Christianity of my story seemed self-evident. I had never really questioned it in all my theological education, right up through my doctorate in ministry. "What are the essential Christian truths you mean?"

"Sin. Redemption. Grace. You sound like a pagan. What about the primacy of Christ over nature?"

"What about the Incarnation?"

Perhaps the issue is perspective. Maybe we are simply looking from different angles. Certainly embodiment is crucial here. Earth, nature, creation are all crucial. The original goodness of creation is crucial. The meek will inherit the earth. How can Jesus have called such an inheritance a beatitude, a blessing, unless the earth is good?

DISCIPLINES OF A SEXUAL SPIRITUALITY

Every aspect of spirituality requires the practice of disciplines. A discipline, as mentioned above, is a listening. A discipline is a focus of one or more facets of a person toward a desired awareness of reality. A discipline is a concentration, a bringing of one's diverse energies toward a center of vitality.

Some of the more common and traditional disciplines of spirituality include using a mantra to increase awareness of the presence of the Holy, focusing on breath to prepare for inspiration, fasting to purify one's intentions from egocentricity, alms-giving to recognize our common poverty and to celebrate that all of life is a gift. Each discipline unites material and spiritual, body and soul.

The action of discipline without the intention that motivates it renders it empty and useless. The intention that never results in action soon fades. True disciplines of spirituality are not dualistic. There are varieties of sexual experience. Each has its own particularities of practice and variations of discipline.

Much has been written, particularly by Roman Catholic authors, about spiritual disciplines associated with celibate sexual expression. I will not address those disciplines here.

Some of these ideas will apply to every woman, but I address primarily the woman who lives in a committed heterosexual relationship. I will not specifically address the spirituality of sexual practice for the single woman or the lesbian woman. I encourage single and lesbian women to articulate the unique beauty of their sexual experience, thus expanding our understanding of primal sacrament. We stand on the edge of beginning. Much of what we dare to say remains taboo for many. But we live it everyday. We must speak.

Now let's look at some of the disciplines through which sexual expression becomes primal sacrament.

PREPARATION AND RECOGNITION OF ENVIRONMENT

The place where love is made is sacred. It needs to reflect the quality of the love, the desire, the communion of bodysouls. Most commonly we make love in the bedroom. As we decorate and care for this room we need to be aware of our rituals of love. The bed we choose, the linens, the number and feel of the pillows, lighting, accessibility of good music, all are important. Sense stimulation in this room is vital. According to your preferences, consider the availability of scented lotions and oils, candles, incense. Avoid anything that could jangle you. The telephone should have a silencing switch. If you have a television it should be closed away behind armoire or bookcase doors. Plan the space to provide you with maximum facility for concentration on giving and receiving the pleasure of love.

I have heard people insist that lovemaking should be spontaneous and not planned. "It's better and more exciting if it just *happens*. It seems contrived or a trick if you plan it."

Only if we are always ready and open to lovemaking as an embodiment of our psychic-emotional-spiritual union with the beloved does this attitude seem contained within primal sacrament. The spontaneity and surprise then happens within the context of an encompassing decision and commitment. Otherwise such an attitude seems to me to indicate a denial of the essential goodness and beauty of sexual lovemaking. The attitude seems to imply that sex, although it is exciting and pleasurable, is probably inherently wrong. We ought not, therefore, to plan for it. However, if we are caught up unsuspecting into the thrill of sexual passion, there isn't a whole lot we can do. We might as well just let it happen.

A spirituality of sexual lovemaking needs to reflect belief in the essential goodness of sexual desire. It needs to be committed to the sacramental expression of this desire, which is connected to a cosmic and even divine desire for ongoing creation. It needs to be intent upon the constant increase of sensitivity in bodysoul of every yearning for creative union.

Often, with regard to environment or sacred space, our attention is not only to the preparation of an already selected space, like the bedroom, but to the recognition of a space that seems to yearn for our lovemaking presence. The place itself stimulates desire: the living room carpet in front of a blazing fireplace on a winter night, the backyard swimming pool under a full moon, a mountain meadow, a secluded ocean beach, a bed of pine needles along a forest path. The possibilities are as varied as your imagination can present.

NAKEDNESS

Woman of many roles, she longs to be known for herself. Complex woman, she longs to be stripped to her essence, her simplicity, her purity of being. She longs to become vulnerable truth. Vulva unveiled. Her truth revealed. Uncovered. Shame-less. She yearns to be seen, to be caressed by eyes that love her, to be accepted and understood.

She strips herself. Piece by piece she removes her clothes, her barriers, every pretense. She watches the beloved watching her. She sees the pleasure rise. Fears of exposure dissolve under his gentle gaze.

Or the beloved uncovers her nakedness. She surrenders to his ministrations. He kisses her again and again during the unveiling—neck, arms, breasts, belly, thighs, knees, feet, and up again into the warm, soft mound. She knows that she is beautiful, simply beautiful. Naked. And beautiful.

Her heart sings:

> O Creator of the earth,
> You who made me flesh
> And found me beautiful,
> I praise You with my body's play and love and song.
> I praise You as warm sleep gives way to wakefulness,
>   and in the dance by which I greet the dawn.
> I praise you in the cycles of blood,
>   in the swelling of life,
>   in the labor of birth,

in the flow of milk,
and in the moist pleasure of love.
I praise you in the good ache
of bending over cribs, and desks, and countertops,
of tilling land, creating art, building worlds,
Of nourishing hungry bodies, minds, and hearts.
I praise you
walking, running, swimming,
dancing, kneeling,
loving on the summer grass.
I praise You that I see the dawning day,
that I hear the cooing of the dove,
that I smell the freshness after rain,
that I raise my voice in word and song,
that I reach my hand to touch, and in my touch
You give pleasure,
comfort hurts,
and heal.
O Creator of the earth
I offer You my nakedness
And sing to You my bodyprayer of praise.

TOUCH

Learn to touch and be touched. Learn sensitivity to the varieties of touch, the levels of touch. Exotic touch of a summer breeze; silky touch of warm southern oceans; touch of a kitten's fur; touch of sunlight; touch of snow; touch of a cool, damp cloth on a fevered forehead; touch of a baby's hand; touch of the beloved's eyes, hands, lips, tongue, penis. Touch on skin; touch into the body's core; touch on the yearning heart; touch on the empty, aching, heart; touch on the searching mind; touch on the wounded soul; touch on the laughing soul; touch on the shy soul; touch on the spirit reaching beyond death; touch on the hoping spirit; touch on the transcending spirit leaning into forever.

Touch and be touched. Learn the loving art of massage. Spend hours touching, in the bath, on the bed, lying on a hillside, bathed by the moon. Meditate on skin. Become aware of sensation, vitality. Focus on receiving the body's touch. You will soon feel it in your soul. Unselfishly touch the beloved. You will soon be absorbed into his pleasure, into the secret reservoir of his joy.

BREATH

Ecstasy travels the pathways of breath. Every initiate in the spiritual life is led to discover the vital connections of breathing to the experience of higher or deeper consciousness. Spiritual guides teach us to breathe into the body's seven energy centers or "chakras" in order to open them and release the vitality they contain. In prayer many people have traditionally emphasized the heart chakra and the "third-eye" chakra. The first is the center of relationship and healing, the second is the center of insight and transcendent vision. Each of us has a chakra we naturally emphasize. Often we associate the experience of the Holy, our "spiritual life," with the release of energy from this center.

"I felt a burning in my heart," confided a client. "I knew that God intended that I work with the inmates at the women's prison. I was talking with this one woman—she had killed her little girl—and my heart opened to her. I felt such power, such love, such expansiveness. I wanted to show her that God forgives, that God forgives anything. *I* forgave her. I couldn't help it; my heart was overflowing!"

"I was meditating one day," related another client, "breathing deeply. It was as though all of me was reduced to a point of light in my forehead. But I wasn't small. I was immense. I was the point of light and the point of light was everything, all of creation, all of space. I was drawn into that light. I can't say that I *knew* something I didn't know before, but I *understood*. It was an experience of clarity. About *what,* exactly, I couldn't tell you, but I felt totally satisfied and content. I was without question."

More and more women are discovering the energy center of their creativity; the sexual center situated approximately at the uterus. When I was young, just learning the disciplines of spirituality, I was taught, subtly, to avoid the sexual chakra. Control sexual energy, I was told. One priest, when I told him of the escape of some of this energy, quipped, "Throw a 'Hail Mary' at those feelings and run in the opposite direction."

Many years ago a friend confided that she had been married for ten years before she was able to feel any sexual sensation at all. "The church taught me well," she smiled tolerantly at herself as she spoke. "I had numbed myself totally. Then, somehow on my wedding night, I was supposed to feel good about experiencing something that had always been forbidden. It was impossible. I had to reteach both my body and my mind. And it took ten years."

One of my clients dissociated her mind from her body each time her husband made love with her. "I seem to be watching us from a vantage point in the upper left corner of the room. I see myself on the bed; I hear the sounds we make; I feel nothing. I keep a safe distance."

A practice of breathing into the sexual center can begin to open us to the life and creativity contained there. Practice alone and with the beloved. Alone, assume a comfortable position, perhaps lying on your back on the bed. Become aware of your breath. Notice its natural flow. Which areas of your body does it seem to fill? Does it flow throughout your body, or according to a more confined path?

When you feel aware of your breath, deliberately move your breath from chakra to chakra. Breathe into the center at the base of the spine. Continue to breathe in this way until that center feels alive and open. Move up to the sexual center. This may be more difficult. Be patient. Just notice how the breath and the concentration affect you. Continue up the chakras: the center of power in your belly at your diaphragm; the heart center; the throat center, from which the energy of giving and receiving comes; the third eye, in the forehead; and finally the divine center, and the crown of your head. When each center is opened quickly descend the passageway of breath, moving through each chakra until you arrive again at the sexual chakra.

Breathe very deeply into the sexual center. Be aware of opening, of expanding. Be aware of every sensation. Let fear flow out of you with your breath. Be gentle when you meet resistance. Caress the resistance with your breath. There is a reason for the resistance to be there, even though the reason may no longer have validity. Let the breath begin to dissolve the resistance. Welcome any images that arise, and allow them to flow with your breath. Do not judge the images. Just let them flow. Continue breathing into your sexual center until you feel open and vital with sexual energy.

Now it is time to protect the chakras. Breathe into the root center, the center of survival at the base of your spine. Imagine it as a beautiful flower. Let your breath gently close the petals of the flower, containing the energy. Then move, with your breath, up to the sexual center. Again protect your energy as if in the heart of a flower. Do this with each of the seven chakras. Then allow your breathing to return to its normal pattern. When this is done your practice of the breathing discipline is completed.

The breathing practice you do alone prepares you for opening your center of sexual energy when you are with your beloved. The deeper the breathing, the more energy you will open and release. Use what you have learned about resistance to be gentle with yourself when you meet with resistance during lovemaking. Match each other's breathing. Note changes in breathing as the sexual energy increases.

Breathe into each other; become each other's breath—an intercourse of breath.

The breathing will keep you in your body if you have a tendency toward dissociation. The breathing grounds you, focuses you.

A discipline of breath also can help us be responsible about sexual activity. Occasionally we find ourselves in situations of sexual arousal toward people with whom we have chosen not to make sexual love. The other person may be a dear friend or colleague, or perhaps even a stranger sharing a seat on an airplane. If we decide that, regardless of the stimulation of our sexual energy center, it is not responsible to engage in sexual activity with this person, breath can come to our aid.

In such a situation begin to breathe into a different energy center, and perhaps use an image to focus yourself. For example, breathe into your heart center and image your beloved. Or breathe into your third eye and focus on the word "loyalty" or "integrity."

By using the discipline of breath we will not experience sexual repression in such a situation. Instead we will simply transfer the center of our energies, allowing the arousal of sexual energy to serve us in a different facet of our being.

BODY-FOCUS

Bring the mind back always to the body's beauty. The mind disbelieves. The mind learned long ago that God is spirit; God is not body. But God became embodied. God created body, and loved the physical.

I watched my first spouse die. I watched and mourned that I had not loved his body more. I loved his mind. I loved the intricacies of his thought and the way he strung words together into poetry. I had not yet learned the spirituality of body, the prayer of the body, the body's contemplation of the Holy Mystery in an ecstasy that runs far deeper than thought.

Once I talked with the spiritual guide, Father Thomas Keating, about the practice of centering prayer. "I am afraid," I said, "that if I go too far in this practice I will lose track of my body."

"Don't worry," he chuckled, "you can't get rid of it until you die, no matter how hard you try."

What I didn't know, and Thomas, perhaps, didn't understand, was that I had not yet learned the practice of body-focus, and that I was in danger of entering so deeply into the chakra of the third eye that I might have lost my grounding in the earth of myself altogether.

Some experiences of the Holy One are possible only through body. The body becomes a sacrament of the Holy insofar as we are willing, consciously, to let body become increasingly alive.

Gently but firmly bring the mind back, always to the body. In lovemaking focus on touch; how deeply can you feel a touch as light as breath? How far into and throughout your body does the sensation go? Where is the connection with soul—how does bodysoul come to be in the act of love? Sexual lovemaking grounds spirit and transforms body. Like prayer, lovemaking is an act of being. Whatever is contrived ultimately fails. The mind learns from the body to let go of control. The soul learns surrender.

A friend once confided in me that her beloved spouse had become her most profound experience of God, and intercourse her most real prayer. She was celebrating the sacrament of marriage. This is the way God comes now. In the touch of flesh on flesh. In the passionate fire.

To increase body-focus practice awareness of all that is physical in your environment. Let it teach you the embodiedness of the Holy One. The swirl of water in the tub, the pool, the river, the lake, the ocean; the fragile touch of rain, oil smoothed on your skin, breeze cooling your perspiration, sand between your toes, sand running through your fingers, dewy grass, long grass waving against your legs, sun on your bare skin, velvet night, moonlight—all deepen awareness of your own embodiedness. The entire creation is erotic, yearning to proclaim in its body the ecstasy of God.

REVERENCE

He comes to me. He, in whom all creation finds its consciousness toward me, comes. He, whose body makes flesh for the Holy, comes. He, whose flesh combined with mine makes prayer and ecstasy, comes. He comes in freedom and in love. He comes with invitation into Mystery, into All-That-Is, into God. This is more than body now, although without body the sacrament does not exist. This is more than the lightning through flesh, more than pleasure's fire. This is the rarest joy. This is the deepest prayer there is until the raising from death.

We enter each other, both gift and giver. Distinctions expand into sacrament as we enact in our bodysouls the marvelous wonder of God flowing through creation and creation flowing into God.

We hold our souls in reverence, our bodies in reverence, the union within our selves, between ourselves, with all creation, with God in awe-filled reverence. We never look at each other without remembering who we are, what these bodies mean, how we are sacrament of a Mystery beyond words. We reach out with eyes, with breath, with touch to glorify God in our bodies. We make love. We expand the boundaries of Incarnation. We continue to create the world.

Your Name Is the Song My Life Sings

Blessed are those who hunger and thirst for justice,
they shall be filled.

NOTHING ENOUGH

Desire for God is an exquisite hunger. Desire hollows a vast space in the soul that will not be filled, for nothing is enough. When there is sufficient silence we might receive words to express our need in something like prayer.

Over the years I have wondered about prayer. I have attended workshops and retreats and I have conducted them, sought guidance in my own prayer and given guidance to others. Yet prayer remains elusive. This I have learned: Prayer happens to me; I do not cause it. I allow it, but am not in control of it.

When she was fifteen years old Kath wrote a poem. I read it because I was her English teacher. I never asked her of whom she wrote or what exactly she meant, but the poem continues to linger in my soul as a poignant expression of an experience of incarnational prayer.

> Somewhere I desired
> to dream of what could be
> of what was not. I desired
> to see where the sun found
>
> crowning, and dazzled all the eyes
> who sought; to see your eyes
> above all not seeing me, seeing
> through me into
>
> a wide and vast space
> filled with nothing enough
> to fill you. I desired to sing
> a song befitting your power.*

Prayer involves us in Mystery. You go along minding the tasks of daily life, being quite common, when suddenly the firm ground slips out from under. Vastness. The ordinary opens out into the

---

* First published in Christin Lore-Kelly, *Caring Community: A Design for Ministry* (Chicago: Loyola University Press, 1983), 96–97.

wonderful. You can be nursing your baby, watching her eyes watching your eyes. You can be weeding the flowers. You can be driving to work, or making a bed, or visiting your mom in a nursing home, or making Kool-Aid for Andy, Tommy, Kate, and Heather. Suddenly it isn't just you and what you're doing. You are seeing through into a wide and vast space filled with nothing enough. "Oh, God!" you exclaim. And you mean it.

My father was a bush pilot in the northern Minnesota-Ontario wilderness. Every day of my little-girl life he flew off in his Cessna 180 over the island-dotted expanse of Lake of the Woods to the favorite fishing spots of his many customers. He was a sky-man. He was a hunter and fisher and man of the woods and lakes. He was my teacher about nature—respect for earth. I look for something of him in every man I meet.

He died in the spring of the year I was thirty-four years old.

Later that summer I visited my mother and decided to take a plane ride over Lake of the Woods. Bob Griffin met me down at the seaplane ramp; he had the 180 gassed up and set to go. I jumped over the shoreline water to the float and climbed into the plane. The roar of the engine drowned all other sound as we picked up speed. The plane lifted. Climbed. The sky is clearer so far from any city, the water reflects its blue. Earth stretches forever.

Suddenly there were no boundaries. Something within me had burst open to reveal the unexpected presence of my father, of the *essence* of my father, in the wide expanse of Something More. He was the sky; I was the sky; but the sky had opened into an infinity of Life so palpable as to be my own body, but More. The extension, though limitless, felt contained in absolute Love. The Being of Love.

"Daddy! My God! Oh, God, thank you." Then it was over. I noticed I was crying.

Earth incarnates the Holy One. When once we have experienced the opening of the ordinary to reveal vast and infinite Love, we live in yearning expectancy. This yearning is the initial movement of prayer. Prayer consists of

> yearning expectancy
> tenacious fidelity
> grateful surrender.

Some people give their whole lives to this yearning. For them spirituality consists primarily in this: to be ready, to be prepared for the visitation of the Holy, to be attuned to the faintest stirrings of divine Mystery in the most common of created things. They are like the brides in the parable of Jesus who keep their lamps trimmed and who wait all night, all year, an entire lifetime if necessary, for the door of creation to open and reveal the Bridegroom of their hearts' desire.

While they wait, while they yearn, they attend to the common things. They trim the lamps, feed the children, care for the earth, observe the changing of the moon, clothe the naked, dance under the stars, give sanctuary to the threatened, receive strangers into their homes, tell stores, make rituals, nurse the sick, keep loyal to friends, visit the lonely, make beauty, make love, make peace, expand truth, help an old man change the tire on his car, help prisoners find their freedom, talk to God simply calling "Father," calling "Mother."

Be tenacious. Be faithful. In all these common things be aware and ready. In an instant, when you least expect, the Holy One breaks through. From whatever you were doing in your faithfulness then, you fall to your knees at the overwhelming wonder of this Gift. This is the instant of prayer—the moment of surrender.

YOUR NAME IS THE SONG MY LIFE SINGS

The times are difficult for women who want to pray. As a spiritual guide I heard the plaints of many who felt themselves wedged between revolving and contradictory images of God/Goddess:

- "I don't know what to call God anymore. How can I pray if I don't know God's name?"
- "Prayer used to be easy, familiar. You might say that God and I

were on familiar terms. I knew God and I knew myself; the world was secure. Now I don't know anything! I'm not sure if the God I used to know is God at all; at any rate, whenever I try to pray to him, my prayer sticks in my throat. I'm not sure anyone is listening—at least I'm not sure *he* is."

• "All I used to have to do was to go into a church. It was quiet there. God just flooded into me. I could come out feeling healed and calmed no matter what state I had been in before. I really depended on that. Now when I go into a church I just feel angry. Then I feel betrayed. Why did God have to be taken away from me? The more I learn about who I am as a woman, the less I can relate to the God I used to know. I think, sometimes, I would prefer the old God to this new awareness of myself."

• "The first time I became aware of the Goddess she scared the hell out of me. She went streaking and screaming across my consciousness like a witch from a fairytale. There was power there, but fear too. And there was no way—no way at all—I could put her and Jesus together. And, to tell the truth, I prefer Jesus. But I let her in and now I have to deal with her. Damn! It used to be so easy!"

• "I believe the old ways need changing. I believe that we need to broaden our image of God to include the feminine. But in the meantime—before we have accomplished that expansion of our God-consciousness—it seems pretty lonely. The old God isn't enough, the new one isn't discovered."

Women have entered upon a *via negativa*—a dark and empty path—in their prayer. Our darkness is a condition of our faith. Our spirituality requires the stripping away of our too-small god. But the darkness and the stripping we experience today is nothing new. Every person of prayer in every era has experienced it. Perhaps we, as women, are experiencing the emptiness as a more general condition, a condition of women as a group, because of the development we experience in our consciousness of ourselves as women. But every person who stands in the presence of the Holy One in the yearning expectancy, tenacious fidelity, and grateful surrender of prayer submits to an essential experience of God as the wide and vast Space, as the Unknown, as the Unnamed, as Mystery, as unending Darkness, as incomprehensible Light. Every person of prayer eventually realizes that any image of God, including the word *God,* is a metaphor that only partially reveals and mightily conceals the fundamental Mystery of our yearning. Prayer is surrender to being drawn into a deep and vast Unknowing.

When a heart attack struck my father and laid him at the edge of death, my mother was troubled. She sat in front of her untouched breakfast, staring out the window into the morning light. Her eyes glazed over with tears.

"Can I help, Mom? Do you want to talk?"

"I don't know what to do," she murmured, "how to pray."

My mother had devoted herself to prayer for as long as I could remember. She insisted on the family rosary, on daily mass, on novenas, on meal prayers, prayers for car and plane trips, prayers against nightmares, illness, bad weather; prayers for friends and enemies. Every night she knelt at the side of her bed ending her day in the calm and protective presence of the God of her faith.

"What do you mean, you don't know how to pray?"

"I mean, I don't know what to pray *for.* I want your father to live; I couldn't bear for him to die. But if I say, 'God, please don't let George die,' is that really the best thing? What if God wants him, now? But I couldn't bear that. I can't make myself say, 'God, take my George if you want him,' I'm so afraid He might. But I feel like I *must* pray. So I don't know what to do."

She had been drawn into the vast Unknowing. There simply was nothing she could do. She knew instinctively that prayer as a means of influencing God was an illusion, it had always been an illusion. That kind of prayer serves simply to influence *us* to remember the presence of the Holy One in everything.

We decided on the words, "God, please give him Life according to Your graciousness." It was another way of saying, "I surrender to the Holy Mystery of Your Will. I believe that You are Life Itself and in You this man will not be harmed whether he lives or dies."

He lived. For two years more.

All those years of my mother's prayer for this and that had been her tenacious fidelity to the presence of the Holy in everything. "Ask and you shall receive," reads the Holy Scripture. Ask and eventually, in a bursting of joy or pain, the vast and holy Mystery breaks through the commonness of our daily lives. Then we surrender, and receive.

Each woman's prayer flows from her particular life, her acceptance of and immersion in her unique destiny. Discovering the way of living that opens her soul to prayer is analogous to discovering the combination of breath and body that opens her voice to song. Although we can learn general principles of singing, each voice and each song is unique. If a person wishes to devote her life to singing, she trains her voice. She becomes aware of each fine nuance of sound her particular vocal cords can produce. She learns to allow her song to ride lightly upon the currents of her breath. She learns which songs belong to her voice, and those are the songs she sings.

The woman who prays allows the Song of God to flow from her life. She believes that God is the Song her life sings.

THE SONG OF MIRIAM

> Miriam, the prophetess, Aaron's sister, took up a timbrel and all the women followed her with timbrels, dancing. And Miriam led them. . . . (Exodus 15:20–21)

Miriam comes forward. She takes hold, envisions, speaks the truth in the presence of the people, exercises authority, leads. At first we do not even know her name; she is simply the sister of Moses when Egypt seeks to kill all Hebrew boys. She watches the princess take her infant brother from the Nile. She quickly analyzes the situation. Miriam comes forward. "I know a woman who could nurse this child, keep him alive; I know where she lives." Miriam sees the possibilities and believes in them, daring to act in a way that brings in the future. She reconnects the mother with the son in the prophetic act from which a future nation rises.

Miriam's prayer bursts forth from activity on behalf of the people. The song her life sings always makes her body dance.

The Miriam-woman comes forward. She is extroverted; her soul expands in the environment of world affairs. She feels the demands of the times and responds with energetic compassion. If no one knows her name she is not insulted. Her name articulates itself through her action, her work in, with, and for the world. Miriam: fruitful woman, she who brings forth a nation.

The breakthrough of God happens for her in the midst of things. Miriam of the Hebrews felt it in the people's freedom from oppression, in the victory of the freedom march she helped to lead. The Song of God burst forth, she needed *noise,* and grabbed a timbrel; she needed to leap and cry out and laugh and dance. The others knew who had led them, and they followed her again as she became the Song of God.

The Miriam-woman is the politician, worker for justice, demonstrator for freedom and peace, organizer of movements, shaper of visions. She is always on the move, and the movement is her prayer.

In a patriarchal society the Miriam-woman often oversteps the boundaries set against women. Then she is outcast, as Miriam in Scripture was cast out as a leper from the nation her prophecy and work had helped to create. Her power and influence with the people was leprosy to her in a social system built upon patriarchal power. She wanted to stand beside her brother, she wanted equality with Moses; she wanted an end to dualism. According to the patriarchal recorder of her history, she was stricken in punishment for her womanly arrogance!

As were the four American churchwomen murdered by death squads in El Salvador.

As was Joan of Arc.

As were the wicca-women healers of the Middle Ages.

As was my friend Margaret ostracized by her upper-middle-class friends for her activities in the peace movement.

But the leprosy itself has become a sign of power; an active reminder to the community of a life denied its song. The leprous Miriam waits on the boundaries of a torn world to come forward again.

THE SONG

I am Miriam.
I remember.

Oh Mystery of dancing stars,
Oh Spiral of never-ending life,
I will be your spiral dance.
I will dance even where dancing is forbidden
I will lead the dance even where leading makes me outcast;
For I cannot live except by dancing your Spiral Mystery.
I am Miriam, oh Most Holy,
I am woman.
Your Mystery is not strange to me:
The sea of blood,
The fiery crescent leading through night
The soft overshadowing of Shekhina through the day.
The milk and honey flow
From your Divine Breast.

THE SONG OF RUTH

Wherever you go, I will go, wherever you live, I will live. Your people shall
be my people, and your God, my God. Wherever you die, I will die and
there I will be buried. May Yahweh do this thing to me and more also if
even death should come between us. (Ruth 1:16–17)

In the song of Ruth opposites come together. She is the childless widow who conceives and brings forth David's line. She is the alien woman from the land Hebrews called "uncertain" or Moab, and whose god was "unknown" or Chemosh; yet from her was descended Jesus, the Messiah. Her prayer, which reconciles opposites, is companionship.

Companion: *com,* together and *panis,* bread. The companion shares bread with another. In the fields of Israel during the first harvest after famine, Ruth gleans wheat for the making of bread. She shares bread with Naomi as her mother-in-law shares life, home, land, and God with Ruth. The prayer of companionship, sharing bread, releases the Holy into the world through a communion of Mystery present in the most common, in All-That-Is. From the body of Ruth proceeded Jesus, the Christ, who proclaimed of the bread, "This is my Body." In the breaking and sharing of bread he revealed his resurrection on the road to Emmaus. The Mystery continues through the ages. Bread represents whatever is most common, most essential, most necessary to life itself. It is so simple as to be almost overlooked unless it is missing. Without it we cannot live long. When we break and share bread together we bring about companionship, extend life, and reveal the Holy One.

The Ruth-woman sings the song of bread. Her God is revealed in the eyes of the ones she companions. She is woman of the hearth incarnating in her life and work that first awareness women ever had of a Sacredness at the center of the circle of life—a Sacredness creating the circle. God is the seed women planted in primal times, the grain women harvested, the bread they baked and shared. Ruth is the mother of Eucharist, of Communion.

The Song

I am Ruth.
I remember.
I never leave my land, for You are my Land,
Nor my people, for they are all that is born from Your Womb.
Oh great and holy Earth,
I remember you from the beginning
So that everywhere is my hearth and my home
And no field of grain is strange to me.
I will sow the seed, gather grain, and bake bread;
And I myself will be the bread I bake and break and share
As you are the seed and the earth where it is sown,
You are the oven of transformation
And the nourishment.
We are one Body,
The Earth,
Contained in endless Love.
All present and alive in a crust of bread.
You are not Unknown,
You are the Bread.

THE SONG OF HANNAH

Hannah rose and took her stand before Yahweh . . .In the bitterness of her soul she prayed to Yahweh with many tears and made a vow, saying,

"Yahweh Sabaoth! If you will take notice of the distress of your servant, and bear me in mind, and not forget your servant and give her a man-child, I will give him to Yahweh for the whole of his life. . . ." (1 Sam. 1:9–11)

"One day," say the Scriptures, "Elkanah offered sacrifice. He used to give portions to Peninnah and to all her sons and daughters; to Hannah, however, he would give only one portion, although he loved her more, since Yahweh had made her barren . . . And so Hannah wept and would not eat. Then Elkanah her husband said to her, 'Hannah, why are you crying and why are you not eating? Why so sad? Am I not more to you than ten sons?' " (1 Sam. 1:4,5, 7–8).

Mothering is Hannah's song. She mothers radically, becoming in her bodysoul the desire of earth to bring forth children of herself. Her song is bitterness of being barren. Her song is tearful, yearning, delirious pleading with the Holy Yahweh whose name has a home in her as "I Am Who I Am Becoming."* It is when Hannah believes she will become a mother that she conceives.

Yahweh and the Great Mother are one. It is we who have separated them. Hannah's barrenness reflects the divine barrenness of a God separated from her own mothering. Yahweh and the Mother are one. In her mothering Hannah incarnates the motherhood of God. But she needs to believe in that divine motherhood first. Until she believes, her barren body manifests the barrenness of a doubted Divinity.

That which one asks of God must be returned to God. This is also the mother's song. "I will call him Samuel," says Hannah of her

---

* I am indebted here to the thought of Rosemary Reuther: "The liberating encounter with God/ess is always an encounter with our authentic selves resurrected from underneath the alienated self. It is not experienced against, but in and through relationships, healing our broken relationships with our bodies, with other people, with nature. We have no adequate name for the true God/ess, the 'I am who I shall become.' Intimations of Her/His name will appear as we emerge from false naming of God/ess modeled on patriarchal alienation." Rosemary Reuther, "Sexism and God Language" in *Sexism and God-Talk: Toward a Feminist Theology* (Boston: Beacon Press, 1983), 71.

child, "because I asked God for him." What is born of Earth returns to Earth. The Word spoken from the Heart of God returns clothed in flesh. The song of the Mother circles, birthing, severing, sending forth into the Wholeness from which all birth begins.

" 'This is the child I prayed for, and Yahweh granted me what I asked. . . . Now I make him over to Yahweh for the whole of his life. He is made over to Yahweh.' There she left him for Yahweh . . . and said this prayer:

> 'My heart exults in Yahweh,
> My horn is exalted in my
> God' "(1 Sam. 1:26–28 and
> 2:1).

The song of Hannah is that of the whole creation worshiping through the act of birth and sending forth. Hannah's womb is the womb of the world, which is the incarnation of the Womb of God.

> The Song
> I am Hannah.
> I remember.
> I stand on the horn of the Moon
> I increase and grow round
> I pull and release the tides
> I am what I am becoming.
> I am water and I am blood
> The Mysteries of the Mother,
> Birthing.
> I carry the future in my belly
> Ripening.
> I sever the cord
> Myself.

THE SONG OF SARAH

God has given me cause to laugh. (Genesis 21:6)

Sarah comes out of the primal world of woman, princess-daughter of Inanna/Ishtar, goddess of love and of the evening star.

She journeys from Ur, the primal place—navel of the earth, attached by the cord of memory to the womb of the Great Mother. Sarah mediates between two worlds, two eras, two ways of thought and being. She, the priestess of the Goddess, stands in equality beside Abraham, her half-brother-spouse and first of the Patriarchs.

Sarah never forgets who she is. She speaks her mind and follows the instincts of her heart. In dangerous times she dons her priestly robes and as "Abraham's sister" and priestess of Inanna visits an enemy king. There as representative of Inanna she enacts the ritual of *hieros gamos* (sacred marriage). Her people pass safely through.

She confounds the scriptural writers. Patriarchy forgets what she is and so misinterprets what she does. Patriarchy denies the women's mysteries she serves but cannot deny her influence and her power.

She confounds a dualistic world. She is priestess of the Goddess and wife of the patriarch. Her priesthood is always that of the *hieros gamos,* bringing the opposites together. Hers is the sacred intercourse of earth with sky, body with spirit, feminine with masculine, intuition with logic, love with law, the Great Mother with the Heavenly Father, the Goddess with Yahweh, Inanna with the Christ. She seeks not to understand the mystery of this union, but to celebrate it.

And so she laughs that the aged priestess of the Old Mysteries of the Mother should give birth to the first son of patriarchy. And she names her son after the laughter arising out of the paradox he embodies. She plants the seed of her laughter at the heart of patriarchy knowing that one day we will hear it again, and will remember the Womb from which we came.

THE SONG

I am Sarah.
I remember.
My laughter is my song:
It cannot be silenced
It cannot be denied.
I garb myself in priesthood
I mediate the Mysteries of Life;
My liturgy is laughter.
I will laugh forever
For this present age

Arose from a union
To which it will return.
I am the laughter of the Goddess
Planted in the souls of all my sons.
If all my daughters will laugh out loud,
Then all my sons will hear.

MOON SONG WOMEN

Tonight is full moon. Each warm summer night for two weeks I have been drawn outside to stand in the glow of her ripening. It is said that women's bodies were once so attuned to cosmic rhythms that every woman in the village would ovulate at full moon and menstruate when the moon was dark. Before we submitted to mechanical rhythms the rhythms of all nature were one.

The breeze is still. Moonlight casts shadows around the curves of the feminine hills. John comes quietly to stand beside me. "Your body looks beautiful in moonlight," he murmurs. The earth. The moon. The body. The rhythms and phases of womanworld.

The moon is the cosmic aspect of womancycles, of the phases of womanbody and womansoul. She is fullness and emptiness completing each other. We learned from the beginning, watching her, that the circle continues: What is full spills over and what is empty becomes a container for the new.

John circles me with his arm. "You came to me when the moon was new. Look at her now."

The moon also brings me to myself.

And her constant transforming brings me to God.

Regardless of our individual focus in life—that song that each of us embodies and through which the Holy Mystery of All is manifest in creation—we will experience life in phases. We will feel the energies of increase and decrease. We will be Moon-Song-Women. The moon is an icon of womanprayer. By observing her carefully we can enter into and become aware of that Mystery from whom all creation is born. By realizing the Song of the Moon in our lives we become prayer; we incarnate (make conscious) what creation has always unconsciously been—the Body of God.

The moon unites opposites; demonstrates to us every night that what seems strangest is really only the other side of what is familiar. We talk about things being at "opposite poles," which in our customary linear thought often means "at the farthest point away on a straight line with no possibility of connection." In spherical thought everything, even what we experience as opposites, interpenetrates everything else in the sphere. All is a whole. But the moon also demonstrates that only one facet of a sphere can be seen at a given time. So we experience life in phases—ourselves in phases, the cosmos in phases, and God in phases. Nevertheless, intense contemplation on any one phase will bring an awareness of the sphere, like the New Moon, which seems to be holding the shadow of the Full Moon in her crescent.

The moon's song is a calling. In fullness she yearns for the dark side, the turning, the coming of crescents. She is whole only in the turning, the becoming. In her calling song she hears the echo of what has been and the murmur of what she will become. The depth of light is darkness, and the depth of darkness is light.

Her motion is cosmic. It is the rhythm of life. It is the pulsing from the heart of God. Our bodysouls take up her song, praying a moonsong in the presence of the Mystery of All.

THE SONG

Moonmaker, Holy One:
You have created me woman;
You have fashioned my body after the turning of the moon;
You have placed in my soul her yearning call;
By the song my life sings, be Incarnate and be praised:
By the dark of the moon
Turning, yearning, calling to the full;
By full moon echoing back the darkness song
In this song my life sings:
   Be Incarnate and be praised!
By the ebbtide
Turning, yearning, calling to the floodtide;
By the floodtide echoing back the ebbtide's song
In this song my life sings:
   Be Incarnate and be praised!
By the bone-starkness

Turning, yearning, calling to the lushness of the flesh;
By flesh-lushness echoing back bone-stark's song
In this song my life sings:
    Be Incarnate and be praised!
By the red blood flow
Turning, yearning, calling to the fertile flow of white;
By white fertile flow echoing back the red blood's song
In this song my life sings:
    Be Incarnate and be praised!
By the self-cocooning
Turning, yearning, calling to an unfurling self;
By self-unfurling echoing back the self-cocooning's song
In this song my life sings:
    Be Incarnate and be praised!
By passion
Turning, yearning, calling to compassion;
By compassion echoing back my passion's song
In this song my life sings:
    Be Incarnate and be praised!
By silence
Turning, yearning, calling for the word;
By my speaking echoing back a silent song
In this song my life sings:
    Be Incarnate and be praised!
By detachment
Turning, yearning, calling for surrounding love;
By my every love echoing back detachment's song
In this song my life sings:
    Be Incarnate and be praised!
By dreams
Turning, yearning, calling for the real;
By everyday reality echoing back the dreamer's song
In this song my life sings:
    Be Incarnate and be praised!
By quiet courage
Turning, yearning, calling for fragility;
By the fragile echoing back a courage song
In this song my life sings:
    Be Incarnate and be praised!
By tenacity
Turning, yearning, calling for surprise;

By life's surprises echoing back tenacious song
In this song my life sings:
   Be Incarnate and be praised!
By stillness
Turning, yearning, calling for dance;
By dance echoing back a stillness song
In this song my life sings:
   Be Incarnate and be praised!
By separation
Turning, yearning, calling for the whole;
By wholeness echoing back our separation song
In this song my life sings:
   Be Incarnate and be praised!
By the piercing stars
Turning, yearning, calling for the glowing moon;
By the moon echoing back the starlight's song
In this song my life sings:
   Be Incarnate and be praised!

YOUR NAME

Either the name of the Holy One doesn't matter, or nothing matters more. "How can I pray if I don't know God's name anymore?" ponders the woman. In *Laughter of Aphrodite,* Carol Christ proclaims, "not until I said 'Goddess' did I realize that I had never felt fully included in the fullness of my being as *woman* in masculine or neuterized imagery for divinity."*

That which we have named "God" is the indefinable Mystery at the source of whatever we can define. So whatever name we whisper will be a fragile utterance unable to comprehend the Mystery we desire to address. Nevertheless the name we choose to speak matters. That name matters because out of that Name (which *we*

---

* Carol Christ, *Laughter of Aphrodite: Reflections on a Journey to the Goddess* (San Francisco: Harper & Row, 1987), 67.

create) springs our individual or communal or national or world definition.

Each creature gives a name to Ultimate Mystery by its unique being. Some names are more comprehensive than others. Jesus is such a one. But the name of each of us, offered to the Mystery, is a prayer by which a facet of All-That-Is returns to Divine Oneness.

I need many names for the Divine One. Each name brings to focus in reality some aspect of the human be-ing, or even the being of cosmic creation, in relationship with that particular name. Whenever I limit the Divine One to *one* name I limit my own reality, for creation speaks the Divine in marvelous multiplicity. Everything names the Holy One—the earth herself, the moon, the morning star, the mountain, ocean, cave, oak tree, eagle, dove, bee, hummingbird and flower, the woman and the man. All creation becomes Incarnation to those who are aware.

Although we come to the Holy One through any and each name somewhat differently, the destination we reach is One and contains the wholeness.

The destiny of Christian women in this age is to return to our Christian tradition an essential facet and name of the Holy One. This is the name of Goddess. Jesus experienced her in his own soul. "I have longed," he mourned, "to gather you to me, like a mother . . ." His followers recognized her presence in Jesus, the Christ. Scriptures written many years later are filled with symbolic vestiges of her in descriptions of him. Nevertheless, consciousness of Goddess was lost to us early in the Christian experiment. She probably was lost because of fear, misunderstanding, a greed for power, a determination to conform to the present world order for survival's sake.

What we lost was the Divine Feminine. It is the destiny of women today to restore this Lost Sacral Identity, this Hidden Holiness, this Divine Sophia/Wisdom who was in the beginning, is now and ever shall be incarnate in Jesus, the Christ.

The world is turning, yearning, calling for her in us. The world is wanting to remember. Our own yearning to speak her name is the prayer of our times . . . to speak her name and to speak the name of the Christ and to discover no division there. Christ turns, yearns, calls Sophia in our souls. Our listening to his voice call and her response within us is the prayer of our times.

Your name is the song my life sings. When I cry "Goddess" it is Christ within me singing. When I pray "Christ" it is the Goddess's call.

BLESSED ARE THOSE WHO HUNGER AND THIRST FOR JUSTICE

When we pray we open ourselves to the hunger of all creation. We agree to feel in our most fundamental being the yearning and calling of All-That-Is for that which alone can satisfy. We experience in our individual soulbodies the collective and even the cosmic labor to bring forth an Incarnation befitting the Holy Mystery.

Catherine, a friend, colleague, and client of mine, provided spiritual guidance to numerous women. She once came to me with a series of dreams that seemed to reach beyond the scope of her individual life, dreams in which a woman was enduring unspeakable losses. In one dream the woman loses her dearest sister and friend in a labyrinth; in another she loses her daughter down a deep well; in a third her mother dies of a lingering and debilitating illness; and in a final dream the woman herself is placed in a concentration camp where she is forbidden all food. Over the door is a sign:

> Take and Eat
> This is My Body

Catherine had awakened trembling and mystified.

"I really think," she confided the next time we were together, "that these dreams are not about me, alone. I suspect I have taken in the pain of my clients—their losses, their struggles for authenticity, wholeness—I don't know—their struggle to hold on to themselves in this culture, in these times; their struggle not to be lost. And maybe it is more than that, too. Maybe the world dreams through us sometimes. Maybe all creation has lost too much, has lost the sisters and daughters and mothers too often. Maybe we need to concentrate on what we need, what we hunger for. Maybe the only food that can keep us alive is the Body of Christ; and maybe that is us. I mean, could it be that in losing womanpower and womanbeing we have also lost the fullness of what it means to be Christ? Could it be that Christ hungers in us for the lost feminine?"

I was reminded of Catherine recently when reading *An Interrupted Life: The Diaries of Etty Hillesum 1941–43*. Etty, a young Jewish woman who died at Auschwitz in November 1943, also speaks of the individual soul as a container for struggles of world or cosmic proportions. She also believes that what happens within her belongs to something greater; and that whatever she as an individual does creatively, positively influences the whole. She writes:

I believe that I know and share the many sorrows and sad circumstances that a human being can experience, but I do not cling to them, I do not prolong such moments of agony. They pass through me, like life itself, as a broad, eternal stream, they become part of that stream, and life continues. And as a result all my strength is preserved, does not become tagged on to futile sorrow or rebelliousness.

. . . ought we not, from time to time, open ourselves up to cosmic sadness? One day I shall surely be able to say to Ilse Blumenthal, "Yes, life is beautiful, and I value it anew at the end of every day, even though I know that the sons of mothers, and you are one such mother, are being murdered in concentration camps." And you must be able to bear your sorrow; even if it seems to crush you, you will be able to stand up again, for human beings are so strong, and your sorrow must become an integral part of yourself, part of your body and your soul, you mustn't run away from it, but bear it like an adult. Do not relieve your feelings through hatred, do not seek to be avenged on all German mothers, for they, too, sorrow at this very moment for their slain and murdered sons. Give your sorrow all the space and shelter in yourself that is its due, for if everyone bears [her] grief honestly and courageously, the sorrow that now fills the world will abate. But if you do not clear a decent shelter for your sorrow, and instead reserve most of the space inside you for hatred and thoughts of revenge—from which new sorrows will be born for others—then sorrow will never cease in this world and will multiply. And if you have given sorrow the space its gentle origins demand, then you may truly say: life is beautiful and so rich. So beautiful and so rich that it makes you want to believe in God.*

---

* Etty Hillesum, *An Interrupted Life: The Diaries of Etty Hillesum 1941–43* (New York: Pocket Books, 1983), 100–101.

Those who hunger and thirst for justice shall be filled, and the filling shall not appease the hunger nor slake the thirst. Instead this divine Fullness will expand our hearts to desire a justice that is greater yet. This Fullness will create that space in us in which the losses and sorrows of a broken world can be contained and transformed. "When I suffer for the vulnerable," writes Etty at the end of her life, "is it not for my own vulnerability that I really suffer? I have broken my body like bread and shared it out among [the people]. And why not, they were hungry and had gone without for so long. . . . We should be willing to act as a balm for all wounds."*

All prayer ultimately hollows our lives into a cup to collect the blood of a torn world and transform it into the wine of justice. Jesus' hunger and thirst led him to the Garden of Gethsemane, where he prayed he would not need to be the cup, he would not need to break his body like bread and share it out. But his lifelong hunger and thirst had already filled the cup of his being with Justice for the people. A life of prayer had confirmed him in his destiny. His life, his prayer, and his destiny were one. He is the Cup. He is the Bread. He is the Wine.

So, too, is WomanChrist.

I DESIRED TO SING A SONG
BEFITTING YOUR POWER

I look at the night sky. It is dark of the moon and the stars captivate me with their clear sharpness. Night wraps me; I feel quiet and without thought—simply held. One time, several years ago, my friend Lyn sat listening to me question the Holy One. Who was he? What did he want of me? How should I pray? What method should

---

* *Ibid.*, 242–43.

I use? What should I call him? Finally she said quizzically, "What difference does it make?"

"What?" My serious mood was insulted.

"What difference does it make whether or not you are in control of God?"

"I wasn't trying to be in control of God."

"I think you were. Why can't you just trust God to be God, and take care of *you*? Why can't your spirituality be to *lean* into God. Let God hold you up for a change. You could even forget about God for a while if you had enough faith and trust. I mean, do you think you have to be thinking about God all the time or God will stop being? Let God do the thinking about you. Let God hold you. God is going to do that anyway."

Tonight her words come back. I am held in the arms of night. I am in the Mother's arms, resting, drifting on the edge of dreams, safe. She is the night and more than the night. She is this wrapping round my bodysoul; she is the soft darkness within my soulbody. She is the space for my dreams. She is the humming of the stars. And she is More. Always More. She will not lose me; I can sleep and she watches. I can wander into the darkness and she still surrounds me, mothering me with gentle safety. She is the source of life and the vastness from which is born the Light, the Morning Star. All I need to do to please her is to be.

Prayer is more intimate and personal than anything because it is not so much something we do, as it is someone that we are. Prayer is our return to the Holy One. "What shall I return to God for all that has been given me?" sings the Psalmist. "The cup of salvation I will take and call upon God's Name" (Ps. 116:12–13 NAB. Paraphrased). I will *be* the cup as I drink from the cup. I will pour myself out into the life I have received. I will be who I am destined to be, and by being, return the gift to the Creator of All. This song heals creation. This is a salvation song.

In prayer Justice is done. Justice is the song of being—being pure, without lies; being whole without subjugation; being simple, without duplicity—a song the fullness of which is the blessing of God. This blessing is the power of life: of increase and the external spiral through death to further birthing; and the power of love: of endless outpouring in freedom and joy into All-That-Is. Prayer is fullness of Life.

So shall I sing my song. The melody winds through creation and forms the Name of deepest Mystery and Being. The Name is Goddess and is God, is unspeakable and as simple as the bee and the hummingbird and flower, is as constant and as changing as the cosmos. The Name is Now.

With each moment the song is new. Each call of the Holy in and to me releases a surprise of melody I never knew I knew before. I didn't. Awareness. The Holy One makes all things new—always, all ways, now. I must be attentive to my singing. I am new. I can always be a song fuller than could be imagined yesterday. I sing my life and I sing the creation.

Your Name is the song.

Weaving Women

Blessed are the merciful,
they shall obtain mercy.

STORY WEAVING

I tell my story. That's what women do. We weave stories hoping to find in the telling some hint, some revelation of who we are, were, are becoming. I read the story I tell and am amazed *that* I remember, and *how* I remember. I tell the story as it happened, must have happened; but I feel it differently now, and I wonder if what I tell is true at all or if, because I tell it from my present perspective, the truth is transformed through the living of it. I tell the past out of the present that I have become.

The story is a weave of women. Mother. Grandmother. Sister. Soul Guide. Friends of many faces. Intimate enemies.

Together we women spin a world web, and on the silken threads of our entwined souls slip toward the center of life. Our web forms a mandala-flower with pathways inward to the source of life and outward to the edges of possibility.

The stories that I weave create a web with other women's stories and together we form patterns reaching deeper than our souls and further than forever. Our lives interweave, providing one another with access to the deepest beauty and truth. We call one another to traverse delicate threads of pain in hidden caverns of mind and heart to find a source and center of healing. And sometimes we entangle and entrap one another with our needs.

I tell my story because that is what women do. In my telling, each woman who has joined her weaving with mine appears altered from who she is to herself because this is my perspective on the pattern. She becomes transformed by the surroundings of my soul. She is no longer simply herself, as I am no longer simply who I am; instead we are the weave. She has her own weaving where her perspective transforms me.

In the world-weave of women we probably wouldn't recognize ourselves. Each of us lives a life outside herself, in the patterns of many others, in a Cosmic Pattern, of which we're often unaware. Each of us is more than she knows.

So mercy. Mercy where the threads of our lives touch and cross. Mercy where we wind round one another. Mercy in our twistings, minglings, changings of color and texture. Mercy where we clash and where we meld. Mercy is the weaver, the designer of the web, and the revealer of the pattern.

MOTHER

The mother is first. Thread is strung long and wound so that always something of her—some color, texture coarse or fine—affects the weave. I have read the books about the mothers holding their daughters back. Back from strength, back from making a name, back from life. In 1796 London, Mary Lamb killed her mother for enforcing her brother's supremacy. Charles Lamb must be free to develop his talents at the cost of his sister's suppression. Mary, despite her own literary abilities was required to support the family by taking in sewing. After the murder the authorities declared the daughter insane for her outrageous revolt. She was. Suppression had made her so.*

I have heard the stories of many women clients telling of mothers who refused to protect them from violent or abusive or obscene fathers and brothers. These mothers educated their daughters in submission, adaptation to a secondary role. "I really *believe* men are superior," said one mother to a daughter struggling for individuation and self-determination. "I know your father always was and still is superior to me."

The stories wound us all. We tell them again and again in an exorcism of womansoul. The stories keep the wounds open so the pain can drain away. But once the wounds have been opened and drained it comes time for healing. Among women that time is now.

Paradoxically the rage we bear in our souls toward the mother will become enfleshed in our daughters. If we are enraged with our mothers, bearing our rage in silence, turning it on ourselves and on what our lives produce, then we will become outraged with our daughters, who will in turn, be enraged with us. The daughter incarnates what is in the mother's soul. And all of us are daughters. The time has come to feel the weaving of the mother through the

---

* cf Louise Bernikov, *Among Women*. (New York: Harmony Books, 1980), 49–53.

pattern of our souls, to speak her name within ourselves. The time has come for mercy.

The daughter speaks:

Mother. Mother where are you in me? It is hard to find you in the pattern of myself because I keep getting you confused with the old woman in the nursing home—the lost one. And you are that one, but transformed by the way I took you into me, changed by the way your love and pain and words and even thoughtless acts changed me.

You devoured me with your dreams. I was a character in the drama of your imagination. "Go out, shy girl," you whisper. I can feel your warm breath against my ear. "Sing for the nice people; dance that cute little dance you learned at school; act—let me teach you this monologue I gave when I was your age. Don't be afraid." And later, when I was older, "You really ought to put yourself forward more, you know; let people know what you can do."

You are my longing for perfection; my dissatisfaction with what is; my compulsion to do more and be better. You are my inability to accept praise. You watch me from the front row of my life; and I watch you for the slightest turn of lip or lowering of eyes. I know the meaning of your every expression and I wait for the one that says you are satisfied with me—the one that always—yet never completely—comes.

You are in the basement crying and I don't know why. I am a child; I am alone. Where is Daddy? What can I do for you? Why don't you stop? You didn't turn the lights on. I am afraid of the dark, and I am afraid of your adult sobbing filling the darkness. The night is the mother crying. This is not a scary dream out of which I can call, "Mommy, Mommy!" and you will come and take me in your arms and murmur, "Only a dream," into my terrified heart. You are the cry. The darkness is your pain.

Yours is a pattern of mystery in my soul. Through the vast tunnel of you I run toward every cry of anyone or anything in need. I enter the darkness despite the fear. I want to heal your pain in everything that weeps.

Don't cry, Mama, don't cry. You are the one who told the stories of life, who showed me where the fairies lived and danced under the full moon. In the winter we made angels in the snow, in summer you picked daisies and plaited a chain for my hair.

The chain you plaited to connect us became stronger than the cord of your own flesh you severed at my birth. We are woven together by every memory: your body warm in the terrified night, each angry scream, each lullaby. The ancient prayers sound with your voice when I hear them echo in my soul. I have tried to leave you, but I never can. I no longer want to go.

The mother speaks:

Daughter, you are my dreams fulfilled. All I ever wanted for you was happiness. When I fought you it was fear in me that opposed your hope. When I pushed you forward it was from pride. Such a wonder you are. I am amazed that everything you are could have begun with me.

But it is only one part of me that speaks. Not all of me has always felt this way toward you. I birthed no sons. Consequently you have escaped the second place that you would have occupied, I must admit, had my son been born. Forgive me. You became my daughter/son: my protector, my way out of obscurity. You would have to do for vindication of my womanhood, and you would have to do by being perfect.

Become my perfect daughter: obedient, beautiful, attractive to men. Remember my advice? "Stand between two blonde girls, always dear—they will frame you with your dark hair and eyes, and emphasize how pretty you are." Support men and sacrifice for them. Be dramatic and emotionally exciting, bright and articulate (but not too intelligent nor argumentative). And above everything, be good. A *good* woman.

Become, too, my perfect son: Succeed in everything. Be first. Never shame me. Protect me, care for me, honor me, make me proud. I want to depend on you. I want your achievements to reflect on my mothering of you. I want you to shine and be all I never could because of my sex. Don't you let your femaleness stop you. Become one of them, surpass them.

(But be subtle. You don't want them to feel put down. Always remember, you are my little girl, my lovely, my daughter.)

Forgive me. Now I see the double bind.

Forgive me; the mother and daughter within me tangled in a web of ambivalence that caught you up in its confusing pattern.

My own mother is tangled there too, with me, with you, with images beyond us all—the myriad possibilities of who all of us might have been had our choices been different.

I fear I may have tried to make you, my daughter, into the mother I needed for my life. The time has come for mercy.

SISTER

The snow fell lightly. When I tilted my head to watch, the flakes dizzied me. They fell from forever, from the very top of the sky. I wondered if it would work to wish on snowflakes. After all, on these snowy nights in Minnesota there were no stars and children had to wish on something: birthday candles, wishbones, a word spoken by two at once, a flat stone skipped on the lake. A spell would be needed, like, "Wish I may, wish I might, have the wish I wish tonight." I closed my eyes very tightly and felt the cool wet kisses of snow.

> "Snowflake kiss,
> Grant my wish:
> Make me good,
> Make me strong,
> And send a sister
> Before too long."

Satisfied with myself I fell on my back in the powdery new snow and whipped my arms up and down to create a snow angel.

"Christin, just *look* at you. You'll be soaked to the bone by the time we get to Grandma's." Mother closed the door behind her and stepped carefully down the steps, which glittered with ice crystals. But she wasn't angry.

Laughing, she reached her hand to me and pulled me up carefully so as not to destroy my perfect angel. "Grandpa says if you wash your hands in the first snow of the year you won't have chapped hands all winter. It looks as if you won't get chapped anywhere!"

The mother and the child I was climbed into the 1945 Oldsmobile and shivered in the January cold as the engine turned over once, twice, and finally defied the twenty-degree-below-zero cold. It started. As we sat waiting for the car to warm up, my mother turned to me.

"Christin, I have something very special to tell you, but it is a secret and you must promise not to tell anyone else until I say it is OK."

"I promise, Mommy, cross my heart." *(Snow kiss, grant my wish!)*

"Christin, I am going to have a baby. Next fall you will have a little sister or brother."

I didn't know which was the more ecstatic, her sharing of such a momentous confidence, or the fulfillment of my constant wish. "Oh, Mommy! Oh, Mommy, does Daddy know? Can we tell Daddy, please?!"

My mother laughed, a delicious loving laughter that circled me and made me feel as though the two of us were dancing with the snowflakes. Then we were hugging and laughing together—"Oh, Christin, you silly girl, Daddy *knows,* darling; Daddy knows."

My father prepared for his son. My mother said it must be a boy since the behavior of the creature within her was decidedly different from what mine had been.

"You must pray for a little brother, Christin. Your father needs a son to carry on. Oh! Here, give me your hand. Feel here. Feel him kick?"

I felt the miracle. I laughed. I prayed for a sister.

The sister is the archetypal opposite: Snow White and Rose Red. We have too often agreed to live out this duality and have felt ourselves separated by our differences. We do each other no favor by this agreement. A friend of mine calls it specialization within a family. She says by the time she was born most of the exciting specialities already had been claimed by her older sisters. There was a pretty and popular one, a creative and intelligent one, and an adventuresome one. None of these traits seemed available to her, so she became efficient. She keeps a perfectly ordered home, manages her own business, invests in the right stocks, is calm in crisis, and mourns her lack of creativity and soul. As her friend I can see that she really lacks neither creativity nor soul, but she can't see it. Those are traits in which her sisters specialize.

Mary and Martha, the sisters who loved Jesus and who have been presented to Christian women as models of sisterhood, also seem, unfortunately, to be specialists. Mary contemplates; Martha works. Mary listens; Martha speaks. Mary is intellectual; Martha, practical. Mary's speciality gets acceptance; Martha's does not.

Sisters often get caught in the Mary/Martha trap. But each sister secretly feels she is in the unacceptable position of Martha. If we could be truthful with each other we would admit that we long to share in each other's speciality. The time has come for mercy.

Dearest Sister,

We are wound round each other in this weave. We are the textured thread—flax and wool spun together, silk and softest cotton. We are color combining.

I have known you from the beginning of your life and you have lived in compassion with the sources of mine. We share the same mother-thread in the unique patterns of our individual weave.

When we were young we believed we were opposite and chose to live so. I went to college, you rejected college and entered the business world. I set out in search of God and the spiritual life in a convent set apart from the world; you exploded into the world defiant with an energy for survival and a determination to take up whatever challenge it might present. Although I left our parents, I remained openly dependent on their care; although you stayed close, you took every opportunity to impress them with your separateness and independence. I was passionate; you were level-headed. I tried to be good; you tried to be shrewd. Responsibility became my life-code; self-actualization became yours.

We emphasized our differences as if we were in danger of forfeiting individual existence if we recognized each other's strength within ourselves. We went to such lengths as to stand before the mirror commenting upon our dissimilarity. "We don't even look like sisters. I am dark, you are ash blonde. My eyes are brown; yours are gray-green. Our body structures differs completely. I look like our mother; you look like our father. I am a Klimek; you are a Lore."

Now I look in the mirror and see so much of you. An expression in the eyes, a turn of smile, line in facial structure, tilt of head. More and more our unique selves are spun around the fiber of the other.

No woman in the world shares more of my soul. When my convent world quaked, fissured, and disintegrated, you opened your home to shelter me. The younger sister traded roles with the older. We sang together songs of hope and grief the day our father was buried. We kept vigil during the long sleep of our mother in coma. You held me at the moment my first spouse died.

We have shared pain and joy, the promises each of us has given to the greatest loves of our lives and the births of your children. We have honored each other's destiny, even the choices we did not understand. We have found our fullness in setting each other free. We have found our freedom in combining the fibers of our unique selves into one textured thread woven through the patterns of our lives. Mercy spins the thread.

FRIENDS

Images of women intertwine throughout the pattern of the weave. Such variety, such color. Faces appear, disappear, and reappear. Some only suggest themselves; others have such intensity and repetition that they have become themes in the weave's design. They are my friends.

We have not always been merciful with one another, but we have never failed to be passionate. Determined to survive our second-class status as women, we have sometimes used friendship competitively and suffered the betrayal that accompanies disrespect. Occasionally we have traded friendship for security, or power, or social acceptability. Now and then we became distrustful of our differences or challenged by common concerns and we sadly drifted apart. But while we can leave one another, we are never gone from one another's lives. The pattern remains in the weave. No woman who has ever been my friend is absent from my soul.

When I examine the pattern of the weave I discover different themes of woman-friendship. The first theme is initiation. At each time of transition in my life—when the former ways of knowing and living create nothing, when I need to relinquish that upon which I had depended for security, when I suspect that somehow I am about to break through into a new world of being if only I knew the way—a woman has come into my life to befriend me. She has, often unwittingly, provided whatever I needed for the breakthrough, becoming a shaman in an initiatory rite of passage. Almost always, when the transition is complete, she leaves to become involved somewhere else with someone else. I am left with love, gratitude, and a newly transformed life.

The second theme is archetype. Some women are mirrors for images in the soul. These women, in befriending me, call forth energies and powers of myself that assist me to believe in myself, to believe in the possibility of being all that I am. They are themselves and loved for themselves, but they are also Goddess-women: highly developed incarnations of aspects of the Goddess that are also in me, but less completely formed.

The third theme is companionship. The companion-friend shares common womanlife. This is a friendship of equals that sees the other as whole-in-herself and honors that individuality. Companion-friends support each other's freedom compassionately. They tell the truth to each other with love and are able to receive that truth without rancor because they know it is neither flattery nor aspersion. Often this friendship endures over time, survives distance, and grows along as each woman develops and changes.

Dear Friend,

I write to you because of all my initiatory friends, you remain most mysterious to me. Sometimes I wonder if you remember me, if our encounter opened some sacred door for you as it did for me.

It was 1973 in Minnesota. I was coteaching a theology workshop at the Newman Center on the University of Minnesota campus—one of those six-weeks-of-Wednesday-evenings things. You arrived with a regular participant and sat through the session silently. It was not your strangeness that engaged me with you, though, but my immediate feeling of intimacy with you, a stranger.

Ordinarily I am very shy with strangers and am not likely to initiate any sort of introductions or conversation. But I was compelled to speak with you. "Who are you? Do I know you from somewhere? You seem so familiar and yet I can't place you. Are you from here, could I have seen you at some time? A conference, a party, a workshop?" No. You were visiting from Alaska, had arrived only the previous day, and had never been to Minnesota before. Still the compulsion. I couldn't let you go easily. "I expect this sounds somewhat out of the ordinary, but could I meet you again before you return home? I don't know why, but I think we need to know each other. Perhaps we have something important to share with each other."

We decided to meet for lunch the next day.

"What am I doing?" I thought as I drove to the coffee shop. "What am I going to say? Why do I want to meet this woman?" You were waiting when I arrived. We talked for four hours.

Both of us were on the edge of our lives. I had just left the convent after a devastating emotional experience, which seemed to question the sources of my identity. You had just left a painful marriage after an attempted suicide. You simply packed your clothes, gassed up your car, and drove to Minnesota without knowing why, except that you were compelled to do it.

We stood together at the edge, our former lives having died. We encouraged each other to choose life. We marveled at having found each other. I said it felt as though you had come all the way from Alaska because I needed you; you said that you felt you had been compelled to come to Minnesota because I was there and you needed me. We called each other sister. We laughed. We were reborn.

When we left the coffee shop we agreed to call each other the next day in order to arrange another meeting. You never called. I couldn't reach you. The next Wednesday I asked your friend about you. He said you had received word that your little girl was sick and that you had flown back to Alaska.

I never saw you again. I have forgotten your name. I remember your soul and I love you, my friend.

Dear Marie,

Over the years I have tried to understand who you were to me when I was a young woman. A mirror, certainly. A mentor. An image of womanhood to which I aspired. Often I used words to try to understand your almost numinous attraction in my life. You are my archetypal friend. Our friendship has been the most passionate and least personal of any friendship in my life.

The young woman I was speaks:

"You are Marie; you are all I ever want to be. Your eyes draw me to your side, compel me to follow you. I watch you from my silence; I yearn to ask you every question in my heart, share every loneliness, wander the paths of every pulsing mystery. You are the blessing of friendship, the opening of the heart, the glory of the mind, wonder of imagination, wine of poetry and song. When I believe in you, you are freedom.

"You are mentor and friend, sister and mother, challenger, she who tears down walls, future-seer, walker of unmapped roads, woman of healing eyes, winged woman, lark woman, womangift. You keep my soul in a room with walls of wind and lift me upon wings crying "eee—ahh" against whatever barriers. Through any pain, through all unknowing we walk together daring brokenness, daring the brigand on the road, daring the piercing look, daring the shattering of our desperate fragility."

I dream you still. You are a dark priestess—lone woman in the sanctuary surrounded by red-robed men clucking their tongues. You raise your slender arm, beckoning me forward. I hear the music of earth, I hear the singing of stars; I see you begin the dance of creation. I rise to the dance.

Dear Ones,

You are many. You are as common as bread to me. You are companions over the years, companions in all that is ordinary and all that is severe. Companions in the wonder of this everyday life.

You are Dottie. You are comfort and ease. We are together where life begins and ends; where you create a nest for the miraculous. During your labor with Becky I rubbed your feet and counted the measure of your breathing. During my vigil with Pat in his dying you stood by compassionately. I come to you for balance and rest when my soul is turbulent.

You are Kath. You are question and critique. We believe one another into fuller being. Your truth is laser. You sever me from pretense; from no one else would I rather receive praise. I have never needed you when you have not been there.

You are Alla. You free my soul. You are magnificence and generosity. You see what I need before I am aware of it myself and bestow yourself as a gift to enlarge my life. You are play and imagination; you are acceptance and encouragement. You are the word-weaver and meaning-maker. Even from pain you can spin beauty.

You are Suzanne. You live next door. We watch your children play; we drink tea; you bring cookies at Christmas; Jesse and Anna leave May baskets and run home thrilled with their surprise of joy. On summer evenings we walk up Summit Avenue and wander down the ways of our daily concerns—sorting out our involvements and busy-ness, musing over family relationships, soothing small pains, keeping silence with each other's tears.

You are Maggie, Bev, Carol, Kathy, Bobbie, P.J., Edith . . . Your names are a litany of womangift. Your faces and the texture of your being in my life give splendor to the weave.

You are my friends. From you I have learned mercy.

INTIMATE ENEMY

The enemy becomes part of the pattern to be ignored at our own peril. She is not evil; she is part of us. She is that feared other side of the soul, which becomes manifest in ourselves when we project her onto another woman. When I give to another woman the energy that seeps forth from hatred of an aspect of my own womansoul, she then has the power of the enemy and can drive me out from the circle of my destiny.

The creation of an enemy is a product of patriarchal mind, a result of dualism. She whom we perceive to be the enemy needs to be textured into the weave, recognized as essential to the pattern, or the fabric will be torn beyond recognition.

Beloved Enemy,

To you I gave the power to inflict the pain of my most intimate brokenness. I feared you. I needed you. I recognized your face in the woman who stood in my way, in the woman who ignored my gifts, in the woman who silenced my voice. When I revealed my wounds you shrugged and looked away. When I hesitated in fear, you laughed.

I ran from you. I ran from myself. The pain is my fault. It is yours.

We have sinned
Through my fault
Through my fault
Through my most grievous fault.

Through no one's fault. Fault is an illusion created by the dualistic belief that someone must be wrong in order for someone else to be right. (*"Someone must take on the divisions and run away into the night, into the desert. Pile the pain on her and send her away, or rather, don't send her away, just let her go on her own, prompted by the weight of her shame. It makes sense to sacrifice one for the good of everyone else."*)

You came to me in dreams. Invisible at first, you pursued, intending my destruction. Then you were in front of me, a crone turning a corner and glancing back knowingly, derisively. Finally you met me in the road. You wanted me dead. Your aggression terrorized me. My weakness filled you with disgust. I deserved to die, you said.

We embraced and fought. You wounded me and I gave you entrance through the wound. You never haunted me again.

Beloved Enemy, you mirror the self I would reject. You do not go away. Your face is anyone's. My rejection brings forth your perpetual presence.

We need to hold each other. We need to spin our various threads into one cord the texture of which will transform us both.

We need to call forth Mercy.

UNRAVELING PATRIARCHAL PATTERNS

WomanChrist spirituality requires us to understand its opposite: patriarchal spirituality. We need to unravel the patriarchal pattern, thread by thread, in order to find the themes in its design to which we have and do contribute. We do not escape participation in patriarchy. As individuals none of us preexist it as Jesus claimed to have: "Before Abraham (the first of the patriarchs) ever was, I Am" (John 8:58).

Some women claim that we carry in our bodysouls the memory of that time before patriarchal power. They quote the feminist novelist Monique Wittig, who challenged us to "remember. Or failing that, invent."* I hope those memories perdure; I have hints that they do—hints in my own dreams, instincts, and decisions as well as in those revealed to me by friends and clients. But I am also painfully aware that most of us struggle to believe in these memories. Most of us struggle throughout our lives to free ourselves from the patriarchal attitudes that have been inculcated in our bodysouls since birth: in family, school, marriage, profession, and church.

However strong our commitment to feminist spirituality, we can remain unconsciously patriarchal in our relationships with one another and with the world. Our spirituality requires awareness of this patriarchal tendency. We need to discipline ourselves to critique our assumptions, our tendencies, our patterns of interaction. The touchstones for critique are reconciliation and mercy.

What are these patriarchal patterns? When their themes are given words, what do they say?

HIERARCHY

One is holy. Only One. "Hear, Oh Israel, the Lord Our God is One." He has dominion and power over the all. The goal of life is oneness with the One. The goal is power and dominion. The goal is to be the High Priest or to be the King. Who is nearer to God, then, the High Priest or the King?

Separate them. Give one religious power and dominion and give the other worldly power and dominion. But who will be right when

---

* Monique Wittig, *Les Guêrillères,* translated by David LeVay (New York: Avon Books, 1973), 89.

there is conflict? Who will rule the minds and hearts of the people? When is it justified to go to war in order to stay in power? What weapons can we use? What is an acceptable level of destruction?

Among the people, who is most favored? Someone must be best. What can be done to be best? What are the rules, the rules of the King, the rules of the Priest? Who has more favor, the rich or the poor? The corporate leader or the spokesman for the disenfranchised? Who, finally, will be chosen? Who will find the steps to rise to the top: of the corporate/political ladder, of the economic pyramid, of the holy mountain?

Who has the will to overcome the odds? Who is heroic? Who will be perfect? Who will fulfill the Law? Who will be righteous? Who will possess such self-control as to be fit to control others? Who will give all to win the favor of the One at the top?

THE SCAPEGOAT

We are unhappy with life; someone must be to blame. Who is so different as to threaten my assumptions, way of life, secure beliefs? Who makes me feel uncomfortable? Who challenges me by their being or their choices? Who appears to have the power to change my well-ordered life? Who is my enemy? If we get rid of that one we can live in peace.

Is the child within me an enemy of my competence, my stability, my sense of responsibility? Punish children. Make them victims. Drive them out.

Is the feminine within me an enemy of cool rational thinking, straightforward progress, dispassionate choice? Punish women. Belittle them with trivial work, exclude them from importance, restrict their sphere of influence, disregard their opinions. Make them victims. Drive them out.

Does the stranger within me intrude upon my security? Then the stranger is the enemy: the young or the old one, the white or the one of color, the capitalist or the communist, the conservative or the liberal, the manager or the worker, the rich or the poor, the man or the woman. Punish the stranger. Change them or go to war. Create barriers to their influence. Make them victims. Drive them out. If nothing else works eliminate them, and with them my fear of annihilation.

THE FALL

All of life is a conflict and struggle with evil. Nature contains the power of destruction, in the earth and in the human; it must be subdued. We must rise above nature, become super-natural. With mind rise above matter. With spirit rise above body. With obedience to law rise above chaotic creatureliness. This is our exile. Here we have no home. Death is our punishment and our escape. Our goal is a heroic death. In the blood of martyrs the seed of our faith germinates. Never give in. No sacrifice is too great. All of life is warfare seeking triumph over base matter. Onward soldiers of God, rise up out of the earth, rise up over the earth, take up your true life in the clouds.

UNENDING PROGRESS

More is better. More money. More grace. More production. Never look back nor spiral round. Forget the place on which you stepped to get ahead; think about the next step. Live in the future; decide from the futuristic point of view. You are in control of your destiny. Use all the resources at hand for increase; the strongest will survive and thrive. Those who drop from the race must have been weak to begin with. Bury the waste, the by-product of your progress, deep in the earth or at the bottom of the sea.

These patriarchal patterns sound stereotypical. They are. Patriarchy is a stereotype that exists nowhere in "pure" form. But the inclinations in us toward this stereotype urge us in subtle fashion to make decisions and act out behavior that increase the sin of dualism in our lives and lack all semblance of mercy.

Mercy weaves creation. Mercy is our only choice if we want to survive.

BLESSED ARE THE MERCIFUL

We are woven of mercy. The survival of our selves, our relationships, and our planet depends on finally choosing to live according to that weave. Mercy is essential and deep. Radical. It cannot be faked. Pity will not do; pity looks down, establishes a relationship of status—the one who needs and the one who helps. Mercy recognizes and accepts what is truest: that we are one weave, that everything winding, twisting, and creating patterns in you is also in me and in all. Mercy is the abiding, creating, loving kindness of the Holy One actively coming to be within All-That-Is.

Mercy creates no hierarchies of control. Hierarchy arises when we separate God from creation; when we believe God to be One and only transcendent. Alone. King of kings. Lord of lords. When God is one and separate our tendency is to climb, to reach out across the vast chasm of creation where God is not. We even step on one another to reach that distant One. We become merciless in our striving.

Mercy teaches us that God is one with us. In our midst. The heartbeat of creation. The Soul by which all is connected. The Holy One suffuses the universe, which is translucent with divine Presence; and at the same time The Holy One holds the universe, containing us as if in the divine Womb. God does not stand above us. Any thought that any one of us can stand above another as a controller of that other proceeds from dire illusion, and threatens the unity and continuity of creation.

To be merciful is to live the image of the Holy One within and containing us. To be merciful is to recognize and to love that image everywhere; even where it seems most different and strangest. We must live mercy all ways: toward ourselves, our friends, our enemies, within our social structures. And we must live with such intent that those structures, themselves, will begin to conform to the pattern of mercy. By being merciful we shall finally obtain mercy.

Mercy casts out nothing, but "overcomes evil with good." Mercy perceives the common source of seeming opposites and spins them together into one thread by the winding motion of love. Whatever we discard—of ourselves or our relationships with others and with the earth—becomes indestructible waste just outside the boundaries of our awareness. Nothing that has ever been part of us can disappear from our reality. The scapegoat returns to haunt us in our dreams.

Mercy is the womb that takes in the seed of the rapist and births a child. Does this seem insulting and abusive? If so it is only because our souls are not yet mercurial enough for the alchemy of life. Mercy transforms.

Mercy is "Original Blessing."* Creation is the outpouring of the Holy One, which by its nature and in its being returns praise always. Nothing we can do can change this. The merciful penetrate nature with heart and soul, body and spirit, to discover their accord with all that is. What divorces us from our origins has mercilessly torn us from ourselves, one another, and the Holy One. "Look at the birds in the sky. . . . Think of the flowers growing in the fields," encouraged Jesus the Merciful One, "if they survive within the loving kindness of the Creator, so also will you. You are all one, the lilies, the birds, the fields, the sky, and you, my friends" (cf. Matt. 6:26, 28).

This is not to say there is no pain, no destruction, no evil, no sin. We feel it every day flowing like a virus in the bloodstream of the world. We feel it like a weakening and listlessness of soul. It is a nausea afflicting each individual self. But this sickness comes upon us as a result of divisions, of getting too far away from the wholeness of creation, of splitting reality down the middle and setting it against itself. Dualism is without mercy and will destroy us.

Mercy knits up the soul and makes us whole again.

As mercy returns us to our origins it brings us a simplicity of living. As we regard all things with mercy we learn their secrets and are brought into the Mystery of a spiraling and unfolding creation. The goal is not unending progress in the form or production. The

---

* Matthew Fox, *Original Blessing* (Santa Fe, NM: Bear & Co. Press, 1984).

goal does not belong to us. It is formulated within that Original Blessing that proceeds from Divine Mercy. We need not be concerned with goal; our concern is destiny. Our concern is pattern— allowing the weave to continue.

Creation wastes little or nothing; all is transformed. Matter is transformed into energy that expands the universe. It spirals. The movement of mercy is a spiral; it comes back on itself; whatever seems lost can be picked up at the next turn.

Paradox again. We throw nothing away, but let everything go; and all that we let go becomes incorporated at the next turn, transformed by mercy. Mercy, you might say, is a conservationist.

AN UNFINISHED PATTERN

Christianity should be the communal incarnation of divine Mercy as Jesus, the Christ, was Mercy's individual embodiment. But our record for mercy is not good.

The Christian attitude throughout history often has been "be converted or die." Many died: Northern European followers of the Goddess. "Infidel" victims of the Crusades. "Heretics" tried by the Inquisition. Witches burned. Natives (Indians in the Americas and blacks of Africa) subdued by missionaries and massacred or enslaved or cheated out of their lands and inheritance by soldiers and businessmen of Christian governments. Jews were turned into scapegoats and driven into holocaust. Women and children are "kept in their place" and often battered and abused under the Christian adaptation of the law of *pater familias*.

Perhaps author G. K. Chesterton was right: Christianity has not failed, it simply has not been tried. Merciless "Christianity" is not Christianity at all.

Chesterton's answer is clever but too simplistic. Christianity *has* been tried by multitudes of women, children, and men during all the centuries since Jesus lived. In most of these people I believe that Christianity succeeded. They believed the word Jesus is said to have spoken, and they honored the life he lived. Their belief resulted in decisions to act in ways that would embody mercy in the world. They did what they could to heal the sick, welcome strangers, feed the hungry and fulfill all of what we have come to call the spiritual and corporal works of mercy. They lived the Beatitudes. They did this among one another, wherever their lives rooted them—in their families, among their friends, in the circle of every community to which they belonged. They became a blessing to the world.

Thinkers like Mary Daly, Monica Sjöö, and Barbara Mor have concluded that Christianity, to have produced such atrocities as the Inquisition and the witch-hunts, must be distorted in its essence— must arise out of a destructive mythology. It seems more likely to me that where the distortions occur, even when they result in the evil of mass murder, those distortions result from a lag in evolutionary consciousness among people and institutions calling themselves Christian. Where we have lacked mercy through the ages and where we continue to lack mercy we have not yet become Christian.

Although we have projected much ancient religious imagery onto him, Jesus is not an archetype, not a mythological god-image. He did not and cannot replace any mythology, be it that of the Hebrews, the Sumerians, the Greco-Romans. He does not stand in the place of either the Goddess or of Yahweh. He was flesh and bone, body and spirit. He lived during a time when the evolution of consciousness had reached a critical juncture symbolized by a clash between the mythology of tribal war gods and the patriarchal culture it produced. Jesus lived beyond either of these paradigms of religious and cultural meaning. He became a prototype of the next age by embodying his vision.

Jesus gave no code of laws. Law belongs to a patriarchal age. He refused even to be caught up in the casuistry of discourse on law— "Which law is the greatest?" Instead of prioritizing the laws he shifted the whole basis of human interaction from law to love. He suggested that we live in such a manner as to be blessed or happy.

And these are the ways of living that promote happy blessing: to be poor in spirit, to mourn what is lost, to be lowly and meek, to hunger and thirst for justice, to be merciful, to be pure of heart, to be peacemakers, to love justice with such passion that we are willing to suffer persecution for the sake of making it a reality in our world. (cf. Matt. 5:3–10)

Where we so live we are Christian. Unfortunately most of the world's institutions and nations remain locked in the conflict of myths. Whose gods are stronger? Whose code of law should prevail? So the destruction continues and neither Christianity nor beatitude prevails.

The time has come for mercy. Mercy dissolves our illusions of power over others who really are members with us of one cosmic body. Mercy reconciles. Mercy permeates the boundaries of tribal mentality and joins us to one another at the level of existence. Therefore mercy unlocks the passage to a new age, a new way of being ourselves and being human, of which Jesus was the prototype.

Mercy proceeds from the Holy One through the soul of each individual. It cannot be institutionally mandated. If we experience institutions as merciful it is because of the combined mercy of the people who make up the institution.

The pattern of mercy winds throughout the weave of creation. In WomanChrist spirituality mercy begins among us, in the weave of women. Mercy begins toward myself, then with mother, daughter, sister, friend, and the one who is not really the enemy but rather the mirror for that part of myself or of reality toward which I have not been merciful. From the weave of women mercy will extend to our fathers, husbands, brothers, and sons.

Divine Wisdom is recognized by the attribute of mercy. She is loving-kindness— the beckoning of Holy Creative Mystery within us. She is the heart of WomanChrist. Mercy cannot be repressed forever, and out of her beatitude a new pattern will form. From Wisdom's merciful weaving true Christianity is, even now, taking shape in the world.

PRAYER FOR MERCY

O Holy One of Mercy,
You who know so well

and hold so tenderly
    The bird fallen from the nest,
    The flower crushed underfoot,
    The wheat plagued by draught,
    The small boat tossed upon waves,
    The child blind from birth,
    The old woman forgetful of her daughter's name,
    The friend speaking false without thought,
    The lover absorbed in her own pain,
    The teacher caught in ignorance,
    The leader afraid to serve,
Hold us all today.
Keen is the pain of our life's flaw,
Awful, the tear in this fabric of creation,
Making us strangers to ourselves.
Flow through the rip in our souls with Your healing Love,
In the emptiness of our hearts
Sing Your creation song
Of Mercy.

Pearl from the Living Sea

Blessed are the pure of heart,
they shall see God.

ISLAND IN THE SEA

$\mathbf{S}$ome years ago I had a dream that moved me deeply and encouraged me toward choices that would result in a way of life characterized more by creative self-actualization than by goal-oriented production:

I am on a journey. My boat sails alone over a wide sea. In the distance rises an island. I am so intrigued by its sheer cliffs of rock and by the way the moon sets it gleaming like alabaster, that I set sail toward it. The ocean waves have formed a cove with a sandy beach where I anchor my boat and swim ashore.

At first I can find no way into the center of the island because of the cliffs, which are perpendicular to the sea and polished smooth by the wind. Finally I notice a path that winds labyrinth-like around the cliffs.

As I travel through the labyrinth the rock island becomes a majestic palace with rooms containing what must be the world's greatest works of art—from ancient to future times. I am filled with amazement. Finally I arrive at the center, where stands a glass case. Within it is the largest pearl I have ever seen. I step closer to look at it carefully and notice that it is alive and pulsing like a heart.

From the watery womb of the Great Mother I am lured by the cosmic moon-woman to the land of "I." I cannot climb the cliffs to worldly success. I cannot proceed through a labyrinth by logical goal-directedness. In the land of "I" every path leads toward and from the center, but the way is one of amazement. The amazement reveals each creation in which I participate and which participates in me. These creations, which in the dream are works of art, have some essential connection to the pearl.

The pearl is the operative image in the dream. Again and again it is repeated in multidimensional representations, each of which contributes to and expands upon the whole. The simple boat in the dark ocean is a shell containing the human pearl. The island gleams like a pearl in the waters of night. The moon is the pearl of the sky.

The pearl itself is the core of the palace of creativity, which is the same as the land of "I." And the pearl is a heart, pulsing life from the center of the "I" land.

In alchemy the pearl represents transformation. It is the "gold" of living matter. It begins as base, as a grain of sand, an irritant, and through the processes of a sea creature's life becomes lustrous and beautiful. In Christian imagery grace or salvation is the "Pearl of Great Price." A hymn in the Hindu *Atharvaveda* exalts the pearl as an image of divine incarnation:

Born of the wind, of the air, of the lightning, of the light, may the shell born from gold, the pearl, defend us from fear! With the shell born from the ocean, the first of all luminous things, we kill the demons. . . . With the shell [we triumph over] disease and poverty. . . . The shell is our universal remedy; the pearl preserves us from fear. Born of heaven, born of the sea . . . to us the shell born from gold is the jewel [mani] that lengthens life. . . . Thou art one of the golds, thou art born of the moon [Soma]. . . . Prolong our lives! The bones of the gods are turned to pearl; they take life and move in the bosom of the waters. I put thee on for life, vigour and strength, for the life of a hundred autumns. May the pearl protect thee!*

In the pearl we are given an image of the spiritual work involved in becoming ourselves. It is as if each one of us is a divine work of art in whose creation we participate. But this creation of self is neither selfish nor isolated. The boundaries of the self extend beyond the individual to the limits of each act of participation. To return to the dream image: Each woman is the "one" in the boat upon the sea; but she is also the sea, the island it contains, the moon that illumines, the pearl that pulses at the center of cosmic reality. Our limits reach as far as we extend our participation. And what we make of ourselves, our spiritual art, finds expression as well in every relationship and in every endeavor to which we give our hearts.

The spirituality by which we make art of ourselves and of our world requires a fourfold discipline: participation, awareness, amazement, and synergy.

---

* Mircea Eliade, *Images and Symbols: Studies in Religious Symbolism,* translated by Philip Mairet (England: Sheed and Ward, 1969), 130.

SHE IS THE SEA: PARTICIPATION

On a dance platform that extended out from her home into the trees, a woman danced the dance of nature. She danced with the trees, with the wind, with the flight of birds, with the swirling rain, with the whirling stars. She became her body. She danced the dance of her blood and of her breath. She felt for how her body desired to move, and let herself be the dance of her desire. After a year she gathered friends to join her, and the dance increased in depth and participation. It became a circle dance moving always deeper to the Center of being and wider in its circle until it encompassed the world. Dance was the woman's art, and art became her participation in a cosmic reality.

Each person's art is simultaneously unique and reflective of All-That-Is. I write, crafting words to form an image. They become a poem or a story. My words represent the image analogically, just as the image represents a larger reality. The individual is like a hologram, both participating in the whole and containing the whole in which it participates. Whatever is individual, differentiated, or discrete is made so by the focus of consciousness; in nature all is one.

Who-I-Am is a choice I make. It is a form of self-consciousness, of becoming differentiated from the whole. Participation is also a choice I make. It is a conscious recognition of the essential connection between the individual and the wholeness of creation. Art results when an individual chooses to participate in the larger structure or form of reality, and then to focus that reality into a discrete object, sound, or action in a way that communicates the beauty and power of the greater reality.

Any work of art becomes an analog for reality by focusing a particular aspect of its beauty, power, and truth into a form. All true art results from a dialectic between individuation and participation.

The depth of an artist's participation and the intensity of her or his focus determine the quality of the art. The quality of both our personal art and our world art relies on a person's willingness to go to the Center. The greatest artist as well as the most authentic individual is the one who participates most deeply and who expresses in word, object, or action those images that come into focus at the Center. Such an individual transcends our stereotypes. We wonder whether to call that person an artist, shaman, or saint. In the lives and work of such people art and spirituality become one.

In the woman is the world. She is the dreamer and the dream; she is the moon and the night in which it glows; she is the pearl and the cliff-castle in which it pulses; she is the woman and the boat in which she journeys.

She is the sea.

GIFT BETWEEN US: AWARENESS

What do you see, dreamwoman? The moon over the island? The moon within the island pearling it with iridescence? The light within yourself projected into the island? If you were without light, would the island be dark? Can you become only what you are able to see? And is your sight a function of your heart's faith? Do you, then, see and become what you believe?

We bring forth from our hearts with the creative power of our belief. Only through the heart flows the awareness that can encompass what is possible at the same time as it acknowledges what is present. "Your faith has saved you" (cf Luke 7:50), explains the divine Seer after nearly every miracle of healing, "your faith has made you whole" (cf. Luke 8:48). The heart sees what has been, what is now, and all that can come to be, "as it was in the beginning, is now, and ever shall be, world without end."

"I see now!" laughed Pat as he died. "It's obvious." And then the litany of his belief, over and over, *"Per omnia secula, seculorum . . .Amen."* And what did he see? Mystery. "I see a Cup with three rings and a Voice that beckons, 'Come.' But another whispers, 'Stay.' I will stay for now." He stayed three days.

What do I see in his final vision? Whatever I can; whatever I expand to; whatever I believe; that for which, at any time, my heart can find the room, the depth, the width, the height, the Wisdom. I see as much as my love permits; as much as there is faith within my heart to see.

What are your visions, dreamwoman? What do you see in the improbable leaves of spring? What in the deep of the moon? When you are startled into awareness by the unprotected gaze of any child-of-the-world, what is revealed in your soul? Does the stone speak the mountain's word? When the gull faces the wind at the ocean's edge, when her wings break into the spray, when her cry mingles with wavesound, when her heart grows large with tenacity, are you aware that her flight is in you and your faith in her?

Whatever we make finds origin here, in the exchange of gift at the center of things. Ursula K. LeGuin tells us in *Always Coming Home* that artists are of two types: those who go to the center from which all life spirals out and create in word, or act, or object what they see there; and those who hear the stories of those who have gone to the center and re-present their vision for the world to see. Each believes in the gift that comes from the Center, receives that gift, and returns it as gift to the outer world.

Only in this exchange of life's gift can we be aware, and only with faith can the gift be recognized. The vision is *received*. What we see depends on the quality of our awareness and the depth of our openness to the other. The pure of heart see God.

ISLAND WE CONTAIN: AMAZEMENT

In a maze we wander, willing to wonder, aware we might lose our way to the way of the maze. The center is the goal, the path winding with boundaries and blocks and passageways. The secret is to go on, whether by reversal or by going round, to find the openness. Attracted by openness we continue until the pattern organizes itself according to our amazement.

The dreamwoman discovers wonders stored at every turn, even where the way is blocked, even where she must reverse her steps in order to continue the creative wandering. She picks up beauty here, truth there. She carries the pieces; they are fragments, shining, meaningless. She cannot know how they fit together—not yet. She does not know that her amazement with the way will lead her finally to the pearl, that living synthesis by which fragments of reality are transformed into art.

Amazement transforms our need to control the outcome into a discipline for continuing on the way. We learn to trust the natural movements of womansoul—we circle, spiral, and come back upon our beginnings; we enclose and release; we labor and we wait, learning to rest while the waiting lasts, learning to breathe deeper than we can reach with our minds. Amazement becomes our spirituality, becomes the rhythm of our breath, the pattern of our moving on. We learn the law of moving where the wonder is most alluring, where the path opens widest.

LIVING PEARL: SYNERGY

Heart is pearl. Within it the complex fragments of our lives come together in an act of synergy—making their energies one. Art is synergistic. The greatest art results from the most complex synthesis. How many fragments can become one being? How fully harmonious are the tones of the symphony? How much diversity of opinion can comprise a political coalition? What is the spectrum of pure light?

We do not create from nothing. Creativity is synergy. The "new" is a combination of already existing fragments of reality into a unique wholeness. What we have is what we are. What we become is the pearl's secret. Some sand. Some flesh. Some tears. And soul. The more complex those fragments of blood, bone, and wave-song, the deeper and more unusual the final beauty of the One Pearl.

Awareness of, participation in, and amazement with each fragment of reality results in our seeing each thing in its wholeness, as it is connected with All. The heart understands that a grain of sand can become a pearl, given the time and the tears.

The spiritual discipline of the heart is to develop a feeling for connections. This is the synergy of human with divine. Here divine Will and human energies of participation, awareness, and amazement unite in powerful and joyous creation. Through such feeling we begin to work our life-art.

Johanna felt connections through clay. Each year she spent a week alone in a natural surrounding, preferably by a river or stream. There she brought together fragments from her life, pondering them, praying by gathering experience into an image in her heart and then allowing the image to link her to what was More—The Holy One.

On the last day she always took clay. She held it in her hands and closed her eyes. Johanna became clay. She rested formless in the hands of a Divine Woman who had lifted her from chaos and was about to give her shape. Johanna held the clay; she was the clay. She became the Shaper and the shaped. She allowed some loving, creating Wisdom to move her hands. She lost the illusion of differentiation. Creator, Creating, Created—and the three are One. As Johanna's hands formed the earth's clay, the divine Artist formed her heart's earth. Later, in the new-formed clay, Johanna recognized herself; and in her heart she saw God.

BLESSED ARE THE PURE OF HEART

Nothing we do is better than the work of handmind. When mind uses itself without the hands it runs the circle and may go too fast; even speech using the voice only may go too fast. The hand that shapes the mind into clay or written word slows thought to the gait of things and lets it be subject to accident and time. Purity is on the edge of evil, they say. Ursula K. LeGuin, *Always Coming Home**

Purity of heart is an enfleshed purity—an incarnational purity—pure *because* it is incarnate, because of the earth it contains rather than the matter it excludes. From an incarnate purity we see into creation itself, to the essence or source or soul we traditionally call God. When we are pure of heart we are not divided; instead we are one with All-That-Is. We are one heart with the Heart of the Cosmos.

Patriarchy presents a reductionist purity when it believes in "stripping away" to find essence. In patriarchy's reductionistic view

---

* Ursula K. LeGuin, *Always Coming Home* (New York: Bantam Books, 1986), 185.

the feminine, as image of psyche, essence, or soul, requires protection. So real women, upon whom patriarchy projects cosmic feminine energies, have been veiled, draped, and enclosed, excluded from world affairs in order not to be tainted by them. But the work of becoming pure of heart is the work of integrating, of connecting, of participating—finding how the facets relate, how the fragments fit, how the fabric is woven, how the diverse particles of the cosmos dance.

Discouraged from engagement with the stuff of life, we are left with a purity "on the edge of evil." It is sterile, and what is sterile cannot create. She who is sterile has no heart for living. She cannot see because she cannot allow herself to be aware of the shadows. She requires no focus and creates no form. She lacks complexity in herself and in her vision of life. Her sterility, being one-dimensional, requires no integration; consequently her life is not art, nor does it produce art.

Our discouragement has cast four shadows: self-limiting trivialization, isolating objectification, paralyzing dependency, and controlling perfectionism. These shadows can cloud the vision of our hearts and eventually make us blind. Purity of heart depends upon finding a way to identify these shadows. When we can see the shadows we can more clearly define the boundaries of our participation, our awareness, our amazement, and our synergistic creativity.

SELF-LIMITING TRIVIALIZATION: "MOLLY"

This poem by e. e. cummings always accompanies my memory of Molly:

> maggie and milly and molly and may
> went down to the beach (to play one day)
> and maggie discovered a shell that sang
> so sweetly she couldn't remember her troubles, and
> milly befriended a stranded star
> whose rays five languid fingers were;
> and molly was chased by a horrible thing
> which raced sideways while blowing bubbles: and
> may came home with a smooth round stone
> as small as a world and as large as alone.

> For whatever we lose (like a you or a me)
> it's always ourselves we find in the sea*

Molly was hard to like. She giggled a lot. She said, "I've never been able . . . my daughter is kind of smart—don't know where she got it, not from me, for sure . . . don't ask me, I barely finished high school . . . a job? Who'd want to hire *me*? . . . I guess I'm good for laughs . . ."

I wanted to scream, "*Stop!* Don't do this to yourself. You are beautiful, intelligent, creative—it's all there, but you are treating yourself like a broken Barbie doll. Stop running from your gifts. Stop hating yourself. Stop giggling!"

Molly was chased by a horrible thing: As a child she was victim of the incest of an alcoholic father. He told her over and over that she was a worthless whore who would die "slapped in jail" if she ever told what she had been doing with him. She believed him, believed that the shadow entering her dark bedroom to rape her was her fault, believed the power that caused his violence was hers and needed to be made small. She believed because he said it, and believing is what children do. She worked to make her power small. She imagined herself disappearing, like Alice who drank the magic potion. Being noticed embarrassed her, filled her with guilt—she was not yet small enough, not yet invisible. She giggled with embarrassment.

She never told until her father died. Then she told at parties, as a joke: "My father was a drunk," (giggle) "he used to rape me at night, the bastard! Can you imagine? Who'd want to rape *me*? He must have been blind!"

I expect I wanted to cry "stop" because I share with most women the temptation to trivialize myself. We need to face this discouraging shadow of trivialization—both in our individual lives and collectively—in order to find who or what casts it upon us. What has stolen that natural tendency to exult in our lives, in ourselves? Or to what have we relinquished it? Where is the courage to cry, "I Am"?

---

* e. e. cummings, *A Selection of Poems* (New York: Harcourt, Brace and World, 1965), 137.

At first the horrible thing chasing us is outside of us, overtly or subtly saying we are not worthy, not strong, not rational, not capable. If we believe it and run we are chased by something more horrible yet–something within: our wasted selves, our potential creativity, our self-limited gifts.

The incarnational purity of WomanChrist spirituality magnifies life rather than trivializes it. This purity is awareness of creation as the Body of God, Incarnate Wisdom. This purity recognizes womanbody as one with that creation. The evil done to her cannot make her insignificant. Instead she circles it, weeps over it, covers it again and again with the most essential *stuff* of womanbody/womansoul—the womb's wise blood, the heart's tears, the mind's radiance—and transforms it into pearl. She is not insignificant; she is sign, symbol, sacrament of the Wisdom of God embodied in the world.

"My soul magnifies my God, my heart is full of rejoicing" (cf. Luke 1:46), sings she who is pure of heart. Mary's heart dared to proclaim her own blessedness for the reason all of us can claim as our own: "The Mighty One has done great things in me" (cf. Luke 1:49). She expands her soul; she opens her heart; she believes the Word spoken into her life, "You are filled with grace, with giftedness" (cf. Luke 1:28–29). She believes in the Gift and her belief incarnates the purity of her heart and fills her soul with creative power.

She faces the shadow; she chases it down. She bursts the bubble of the horrible thing: the lie of false power—power over—power to trivialize a woman's life. She confronts the horrible thing. It is empty. It has no heart.

ISOLATING OBJECTIFICATION: "KARLA"

Last week I received a letter from Karla. I think I could like her a lot; even though I have called her my friend for years, I hardly know her at all. She apologized for having not written, explaining that she hadn't wanted to experience the feelings that might arise were she to reflect upon her life. She did not want to face the loss.

I pondered this. The loss? What loss? Images of her crowded my mind. Memories from over the years.

A mutual friend, Susan, crying—"Karla called me a liar. I do not lie. She didn't even let me tell my side of it. She just looked down at me with those cold, dark eyes and told me I was lying. I can't forgive her. Ever."

Eva, her roommate as a young adult—"I thought it would work so well, living with Karla. We always had so much fun before, doing things together—concerts, movies, theater, skiing, camping. But when we moved in together it was as if I had become her greatest enemy. She came and went without greeting or good-bye. She shut herself away in her room; I could hear her talking on the phone to her friends, laughing, making plans; I finally realized those plans weren't going to include me anymore. But worst of all, when I tried to talk with her about it, she acted as if I were imagining things. She seemed to think nothing had changed between us. Finally, I moved out. It was just too hard."

Karla in mid-life, is a successful professional woman in a position of considerable authority. The decisions she makes are major, and she brings to them a high degree of intelligence, discrimination, and objectivity. She has honed her emotions with fine controls to prevent her own needs and desires from influencing the outcomes of professional choices she needs to make each day. The character she has formed for herself seems perfectly suited to the life she has chosen. Yet she writes: "I don't write because I could not face my loss."

What is the loss? Did the objectivity she seemed to cultivate prevent her from making intimate connections with others? With life itself?

If we objectify the world we isolate ourselves. When we objectify something we cannot see it as it really is. When we withdraw our participation from its reality we take away something essential to its identity and diminish some facet of ourselves that depends on it for vitality. The seer, seen, and seeing are one. The pure of heart see God—in all and always.

Objectification is not the same as differentiation. In creation a marvelous diversity exists. Each of us is unique and unrepeatable. But we *see* and understand and learn to treasure our differences through an act of participation. When we make an object of something or someone we need to separate ourselves from it, set it "out there."

Our rationalizations for objectifying seem reasonable: to be fair to the other, to leave the other free, to limit "subjective" interpretation or judgment of the other, to see the other clearly in itself, to be "professional," to be "clinical." But often our objectivity is simply a cloak for fear of intimacy, or for loss of perfect self-control and control of the situation, or for discovering our personal vulnerability of heart.

Purity of heart begins with vulnerability of heart. Jesus, the pure of heart, stands above his objectifying city: "Oh Jerusalem, Jerusalem, you that kill the prophets and stone those who are sent to you! How often have I longed to gather your children, as a hen gathers her chicks under her wings, and you refused! So be it! Your house will be left to you desolate." (Matt. 23:37–38).

We women have been taught from childhood that our nature requires us to be vulnerable to the penetration of the other—into our bodies and our souls—and leaves us vulnerable to the pain of unwanted penetration. We have been taught that we are the ones with the wound *(vulnerus),* the openness *(vulva);* we are the pregnable ones, open to life-bearing and open to attack.

Here is the paradox. For fear of attack we reject vulnerability. We close ourselves off to keep the "other" outside. We build walls around our hearts and fail to develop the ability to discriminate between the other who brings life and the other who threatens death. We become the walled Jerusalem refusing the mothering Christ in us, so our "house is left to us desolate." Our objectifying isolates us. We begin to grieve for something we have lost, and we wonder why the pain: We protected ourselves from pain; we made ourselves objective and strong.

The interpretation of "vulva" as "wound" and consequently of "vulnerability" as the "availability for wounding" surely did not come from the wisdom of women. In woman the vulva is *not* a wound; rather it is the threshold of life, the door through all new life is born into the world.

Only in primitive males was "vulva" experienced as a "wound." In order to share in women's mysteries of blood and birth, males of ancient tribes ritualistically gave blood to the Great Mother Goddess by wounding themselves genitally. They carved a vulva into their male bodies. They "fertilized" the earth with their blood. Many of them died from their wounds.

We inherit our fear of vulnerability from patriarchal language sources, not from our own experiences, not from women-words. For woman to be vulnerable means for her to be the threshold, the gateway of life. Our choice to open or close this door must be based on worthiness, not upon fear. When we accept the patriarchal image of ourselves as the wounded ones needing protection, we accept a false image. We become merely a projection of the unconscious male fear of self-castration.

The pure of heart live dangerously in this world that values objectivity, rewards the steely eye and the iron heart. But "who shall ascend the mountain of Yahweh? *(El Shaddai, the Breasted God)* The person with clean hands and pure heart, who studies not deceitful things. . ." (Ps. 24:3–4). "Why shut your hearts so long, loving delusions, chasing after lies?" (Ps. 4:2). The lie is the egoism of setting ourselves apart from creation as if all did not come forth from the Womb of God, as if everything is not nourished at the breast of El Shaddai. The heart that is pure is the heart that is open to the flowing of creation. The pure heart feels both the ecstasy of life's increase and the pain of diminishment as the cycle of creation continues. Because all is felt, the true can be distinguished from the false—the true received, conceived, and embodied in the world, the false rejected and cast forth.

We need to trade isolating objectivity for courageous vulnerability. Not the wounding vulnerability that victimizes us, but the threshold vulnerability that opens our hearts to the sight of God. When we can *see* God, we can also distinguish that which is not God. We become clear-hearted.

Look at what women's mysteries can teach us. Look closely and do not reject. The vulva is the threshold. It is a "wound" only because of patriarchy's fear of openness to creation, which led to a misnaming. Vulnerability is openness of womb and openness of heart. Through that threshold love enters and is incarnated in the ongoing creation. Through that threshold the unworthy is bled forth. God is the most vulnerable of all.

PARALYZING DEPENDENCY: "JENNIFER"

Elise says that Jennifer won't have lunch with her anymore. "I haven't seen her for five years. I talk with her on the phone now and then, but it's depressing. She sounds awful! What if she's drinking or doing drugs or both? Probably she isn't beautiful anymore and doesn't want to be seen. Damn! I *love* that woman. Doesn't she know that? What do I care what she *looks* like? And it makes me so sad. It's such a loss. Such a goddamn loss!"

Jennifer was a brilliant anthropologist. Her enthusiasm for her science impelled her always to seek a deep and refined understanding of people and their cultures. When she married a handsome, dominant, wealthy man she laughingly told her friends that he had seduced her with the promise of time for travel and research. She would be able to pursue her science as never before.

The research was never begun, although she talked about it for some years after the wedding. Her husband's business required extensive travel; Jennifer often accompanied him. Willowy and tall with hair the color of ripe barley, she was beautiful; he displayed her to his associates as one would an art acquisition. She was understanding; he began to use her to attract customers.

I knew her only slightly, but remember vividly an event that happened during a company party at her husband's office. Jennifer and I were engaged in conversation about mythology when her husband broke in on us, trailing a disgustingly intoxicated little man. "Jennifer," he boomed so that everyone in the room could hear, "I've been telling Al, here, how sexy you think he is and how you are dying to dance with him." Then, "So here she is, Al, have fun!"

Jennifer quietly began to demur—"Thank you, but Christin and I were . . ."

He pushed her onto the dance floor. She smiled at me a bit ashamedly, but graciously, and turned to the stumbling Al. They were the only ones dancing. The crowd watched. I, unable to witness her abasement, left the party.

After that I heard about her secondhand from Elise. "Jennifer doesn't talk about anthropology anymore . . . I think she is drinking . . . she says she has to take pills for her nerves . . . she sounds so strange on the phone . . . she no longer leaves her house."

The shadows that obscure our vision of God are cast by a patriarchal world deliberate in its intent that we *not* see. Our clarity of heart threatens not only this world's power, but its very existence. The God appearing in the hearts of women and incarnated in our lives and in the lives of our children would reform and transform the most fundamental structures of our cultures and societies. "This world will seek to destroy you," warns the Christ. "Remember you are not of this world."

The most widespread shadow cast upon us by patriarchy is dependency. It paralyzes us and makes us powerless. Mostly we become dependent on our men. The process is subtle, it comes cloaked as love. Slowly, almost imperceptibly, our abilities and powers dissolve: We cannot support ourselves financially, we stop communicating with our women friends, we live vicarious soap-opera existences. We drink, take tranquilizers, or eat to dull the pain of our dying or to fill the emptiness left where our spirits used to be.

Many books have been written on the subject of dependence; the affliction is so widespread, particularly among the women in our culture. If these women are not dependent on some substance such as alcohol, they are likely to be "codependent," meaning that they support the dependence of someone else. My intention here is not to repeat work already done, but to focus on the implications of dependence regarding our attempts to live a WomanChrist spirituality.

It could be that Jennifer, in her decision to allow herself to be dependent on her husband for support of her scientific endeavors, became codependent with him in his addiction to power and success. Her codependence sapped the energy she needed for her own creation. Recognizing her growing emptiness she sought to dull the pain that results when we feel we cannot create. She turned to drugs. The spiral of dependency and codependency has led to stasis, powerlessness, paralysis of heart.

For the paralyzed heart there is no amazement, no purity, no vision, no path to the Pearl.

What practice of spirituality can we adopt if we cannot move? Lyn Cowan, in her study of melancholy, distinguishes between that condition and depression: Depression is opaque; melancholy is lucid. When our hearts are paralyzed from dependency we become depressed, opaque, unable to see. We are not pure of heart. The task of spirituality is to transform our depression into melancholy.

One might compare depression to sinking into quicksand and melancholy to sinking into the sea. Both are a kind of death; but while the quicksand disintegrates us, the sea turns us into pearl. The sea is Mara, Mari, Mere, the ancient Goddess, the womb of creation, the all-receiving tomb. The sea is Mary, "Star of the Sea," from whose watery womb springs the Child of Promise, the Pearl of Great Price.

The dependent woman needs to sink until she reaches her primal beginnings. Depression fights the sinking feeling, fights the reasons for the sinking, fights the self that sinks. Melancholy allows the sinking, lets go, permits the awareness, acknowledges the dependence, mourns what has been lost. The depressed woman focuses on what she experiences as her ugliness, and the ugliness paralyzes her. The melancholy woman focuses on the beauty she once experienced as part of herself, and lets the loss of it fill her with longing. The longing turns the loss to pearl and her beauty returns, transformed.

We need to remember who and what we are. Woman is the sea. In our darkest moments our spirituality can bring us to the beginning of all creation—the image of the feminine Spirit, brooding (a mother on her nest) over the deep (the primal mother-sea). The deep darkness of primal woman is our natural environment for creation. We need not, must not fill it up, for from it is born all that is alive, all that is beautiful, all that is dangerous, all that is pure, all that is free.

CONTROLLED PERFECTIONISM: "BANSHEE-WOMAN"

This woman is not real and she is more than real. She is a dreamwoman, more at the root of the self than the woman-awake. She hasn't a name because she is more than one; she is the controlled, the controller, the attacker and the attacked. She is what prevents the work of art. She is what stops the heart. Here is my dream:

This is the house where I work; all my work comes from here. It is the source, the container. It is large. It is a maze. The ceilings are high. I cannot find my way in the dark.

In a room like a dormitory for sick people a woman is being put to bed for the night. This woman is the subject and source of all my work. I stand in the shadow and watch as a convulsion seizes her and she writhes in pain. People circle her bed and hold her down; they restrain and control her. As I watch I feel her sickness within myself and I realize that I cannot do the work, I cannot take the pain, it makes me sick.

I run to hide from the controlling of the woman. To my left is a large institutional bathroom. I dash inside and lock myself in one of the metal toilet stalls where I perch on a toilet so that my legs cannot be seen. I will wait to be rescued. "I can't take this work anymore! I want to quit. If my father knew how much I want to quit he would let me; he would want me to quit. I'll ask him if I can. But wait! I don't need to ask him. I will just quit."

At that moment a Banshee-Woman appears on the left, above me, and taunts:

"So, you can't take it?!"

I reply, "I'm not cut out for this kind of work."

The Banshee-Woman: "What? Is all your education failing you, then?"

Myself: "It isn't a question of education, it is a question of heart, of the character of my soul."

At that, the Banshee-Woman becomes a screaming vulture and descends to attack me. I put my feet against the door to prevent her entry, but I know there is no protection from her. I scream "No!" and awake.

Control of the woman, of the creative power buried in the repressed feminine, is the work we have been assigned by the father, by patriarchy. Stop the convulsions. Drug her. Restrain her. But the convulsions are the labor of birth, the releasing of control that sets free the first tremors of creativity in the soul. The pain of woman is caused not by the lack of control, but by the imposition of it—by the enforced restraint. Restraint of the feminine, itself, makes us sick.

This dream signals to the dreamer, who has been wandering in the darkness of her womansoul, the dawning of a realization. No longer can she do the work of controlling or restraining womanpower in herself, in her art, in society, in the women and men of the world, in the earth and cosmos, which is our larger body.

Perfection brought about by control of creative woman-energy is a lie from which we must be purged, cleansed.

The Banshee-Woman screaming in our dreams and threatening our destruction represents the irony and paradox of women in our era. On the one hand we women believe the lie about needing to be perfect and perfectly controlled. When such belief is strong the Banshee Woman attacks to taunt us with our insecurities. She represents the irony that our carefully controlled rational and responsible lives perfected by the "fathers'" education "can't take it." When moved by the power of the heart to do the woman-work of creation, our facade of perfection serves us ill.

Paradoxically the Banshee-Woman tears down on us with the scream of death. She terrifies. The perfection we have sought won't save us when confronted with life itself. She is an aspect of the Goddess, consuming the waste like a vulture. In Celtic mythology she receives the last breath of the dying in a "kiss of peace." Barbara Walker reminds us that the Banshee "could bring the dead soul to a rebirth by sucking it into [herself] with the final kiss."*

Here is the elemental feminine, purging the heart of falsehood to release what is real. She is the incisive aspect of Wisdom, swordsharp, piercing to the heart's core. She is the subtle teller of truth. She is the Crone who dares dissolve lies in her cauldron of transformation in order to return us to ourselves pure of heart.

PEARL PURE WISDOM

Oh, Wisdom
Secret of the heart
Creator, Preserver, Transformer of worlds,
Combining in your Divine Art

---

* Barbara Walker, *The Crone: Woman of Age, Wisdom and Power* (San Francisco: Harper & Row, 1987), 75.

Sand and tears,
Shadow and light,
Form my heart in the purity of pearl.

Awaken me
To the wonder of your Being in All and containing All
Awaken me
To the amazement of eternal coming to be
In the heart of the world
Your Heart
Pulsing in everything
Pulsing in me.

Move me
With the circles, spirals, turnings, returnings
Of creation itself,
The cosmic pearl
Of your Body
Shimmering, shining, radiant
In the deep of the Eternal Sea.

Make art of me
And teach me
To spin myself outward into the world
My life, a gift of art,
Whatever form my participation takes.

Oh, Mother of All Being,
Teach me the purity of containing
As You do
All that enters the circle of my life.
From pleasure
Bring forth from me the pearl of beauty,
From light
Bring forth from me the pearl of truth,
From darkness
Bring forth from me the pearl of comfort,
From pain
Bring forth from me the pearl of compassion,
From death
Bring forth from me the pearl of your transforming life

Spiraling forever
Out from your birthgiving Heart.

For of You it is written:
"Wisdom is quicker to move than any motion;
she is so pure, she pervades and permeates all things.
She is a breath of the power of God,
pure emanation of the glory of the Almighty;
hence nothing impure can find a way into her.

Although alone, she can do all;
herself unchanging, she makes all things new." (Wis. 7:24–25; 27)

PARABLE: A WOMAN OF PEARL

Twenty-five years after entering the convent, and eleven years after leaving that institution for another way of life, I returned to celebrate the silver jubilee of a woman who was my friend. Returning surprised me. I thought I was released from that past, had settled the questions, dispelled the dreams. I assumed I would never go back to the prairie community, but would go forward in my spirituality and my life while closing the cover on that chapter of my story.

I was wrong. I forgot that nothing is ever finished, only transformed. Who I am and what I experience and believe of the Holy Mystery always will include those women and everything they gave to me.

As Pat and I drove up the long road I felt my stomach turn with a flow of nausea when the convent came into view. Reaching out my hand to him, I whispered, "I'm afraid." All these years I had lived with this place as a part of me, trying to tell myself the truth about my life here and knowing that the truth is never told really. I had let the pain of its incompleteness pour through me and had mourned the passing of its power to give me joy. I had sought in my present life for seeds of the spirituality planted while I lived at this place, and had pruned the trees of knowledge and understanding those seeds had become. Everything I am reached back to and was rooted here and I felt afraid to know that, so deeply dis-membered as I was. My spouse took my hand and murmured softly, "It will be all right, you will do fine."

He meant the incense. Some weeks previously we had received an invitation from Sister Maria, whose twenty-fifth anniversary of profession it would be. Although I had loved and still love her deeply, I had chosen not to attend because, as I thought, I would not be returning to that place upon which the chapter had been closed. However, before I had the opportunity to respond negatively, I received a phone call from her. She asked if I would be willing to be an incense bearer in the jubilee procession, leading the jubilarians into the chapel for the Eucharistic celebration. A realization of significance beyond comprehension obliterated my previous choice and I said, "Yes."

Pat parked the car and got out. I felt riveted to the seat. He walked around and opened the door on my side.

"Pat, I don't think I can. I can't move."

"Come on, now, Christin. It will be all right. They are your sisters."

The strong prairie wind whipped my hair into my face as I stepped out of the car and onto the driveway. We went through the front door. As I was trying to smooth down the wind's dishevelment I heard the voice of my mentor, Sister Marie Schwan.

"Christin, welcome home."

I was swept into her arms, and then the arms of another and another. All over the voices, "Home . . . Home . . ." and Patrick was laughing and saying, "Yes, we do need to come home at least once a year." It was a dance, a homing dance. Old Sister Pauline held me crushed to her breast, then out at arm's length, cooing: "Little Christin, my little Christin!" Some had never known me; one stared at me and when I said hello to her she turned away deaf and mute; it was as though I were a ghost and when I spoke the spell broke and she needed to pretend there was no one there. I was not hurt.

Each one is who she is, and so am I. We are the circle, I am remembered.

So I led the procession into the House of God. Sister Rosemarie and I lifted bowls of incense high from side to side of the chapel, up, down, around, encircling all. "Let my prayer arise, Oh God, as incense in Thy sight; the lifting up of my hands, as an evening sacrifice."

After the Mass was over and we had led the procession out, she put her arm around me: "I wanted to tell you. When we stood before the altar and bowed, I felt so strongly that I should take your hand. I know it wasn't part of what we were supposed to do, and that was the only thing that stopped me; the surprise you might have felt in front of all those people. But it would have been *right*. It would have meant something that should have been proclaimed."

I went back into the chapel thinking that I would get my purse and camera and then find someone who could show me to Sister Marie Nativity's room. As I was picking up my things, Sister Ann Marie bustled through the door, took my hand, and said, "Come with me." I found myself following, obediently. All at once, amused, recalling that it was not twenty-five years ago, I questioned her: "Where are you taking me?"

"To see Sister Nativity. She saw you from the balcony . . . I pointed you out as you carried the incense . . . She is eager to see you."

Sister Nativity stood leaning on her black cane in the center of the hallway. From behind her the sunlight haloed her so that I could not, at first, see her face. On either side of her stood my friends, two women who were also former members of this community. As I came near and Marie Nativity recognized me she opened both arms, lifting her cane from the floor and leaning toward me. Her face became all light, her eyes shone, and with a voice breaking from age and laughter she cried: "You came!" I bent to kiss her, aware of an overwhelming energy of love and power folding round the two of us. I heard the two women exclaim in wonder, and was vaguely aware of the flash of a camera capturing this greeting. Sister Ann Marie helped the older Sister Marie Nativity into a small sitting room where she and I talked for about an hour.

First I looked upon her age. Frail. Smaller than an eight-year-old child. Transparent. Pearl. Shining. I wanted to imprint upon my soul every gesture, every word. I felt lightheaded with concentration. All else faded into the background while I was caught up in her.

"You are old, Sister."

"Yes. Ninety. But the sisters are good to me, to all of us, here . . . I am so glad you have come. Will you stay here with us tonight?"

I explained that Pat was with me, and we would be staying in a motel. I would be at the convent only during the remainder of the afternoon. She scrutinized me carefully:

"Are you glad to be a woman?"

"Oh, yes, Sister. Why do you ask?"

"Being a woman is whole."

"Why do you say that, Sister?"

"Men have more difficulty. It is so compelling for men to be selfish. They want to be pure. But their purity has become stark. Women give birth. We are of the earth. We feel what it is to be created. Our purity is pearl. Translucent, but full. This purity contains everything."

She turned her face toward the window and the sun bathed her in warm light; her eyes were closed. Then she looked at me narrowly out of the corners of her eyes as if to say: Will you take scandal at what I am going to say next? Then she said, definitely, slowly, each word punctuated: "Everything—created—is—God!"

"I think so, too."

"You do?!" Laughing. Excited.

"Oh, yes. The earth, the cosmos, we are God's Body."

"Yes, yes. God's Body. And loved. God *loves* us; and once God has loved, that love can never be taken away. Even if there is a hell God loves those who choose to be there. God loves them with a pity surpassing anything we can imagine. Everything that is baptized is loved by God!"

"But Sister"—the careful delineations of Catholic dogma were being confused here—"What about those who are *not* baptized?"

She laughed at me as if I were a simple and delightful child and cried out triumphantly: "There *is nothing* that is not baptized!"

"You mean God takes care of it?"

"Of course. Everything is loved of God. Everything *is* God. Nothing escapes that overwhelming love. Nothing is not that Being."

She closed her eyes, then, and seemed to be contemplating a great mystery.

"When I was young I loved beauty, art, and intellectual things—all my life that love grew. Now it is gone. I no longer can remember when I begin to speak how I thought I might end my thought." She paused. I waited, thinking what a great poet and teacher she had been in her life; how she gave substance to both beauty and truth. Then she broke out in laughter.

"What is it, Sister?"

"I always know that what is at the end is God!" Another long pause. "Christin, please promise me something."

"Anything, Sister."

"Carry on the work that I began. Teach. Let the life begun in me complete itself in you. Make art out of it."

I felt the tears begin to come to my eyes. My heart was so full of her and of her mothering of my soul I felt about to break; and now this recognition by the oldest nun remaining in this community of women that I was one with her, and with them. My leaving had not disconnected me after all. Our story would continue whatever my path. Such are the connections between women that reveal the essential wholeness of creation.

"Yes, Sister. I promise you, and treasure the honor you have given me by your request, which is also the gift of your life. Now I have a request of you."

"What is it?"

"I may never see you again." Marie Nativity looked at me wonderingly through her ninety-year-old eyes. "I mean that you are old, and you may die before I have a chance to travel back here." She smiled in agreement. "What I want from you is a message for my life. What should I remember from you all the days that I live?"

She looked at me hard, then closed her eyes for a long time. Finally she said very slowly and with great assurance: "You *are* God!" Then laughing, "You can't get any purer!"

I thought of the many years ahead of me that I would be compelled to contemplate the mystery of her words. I didn't want to leave her, but the power of her frail presence had filled me to such an extent that neither could I stay much longer. This ancient woman gave birth in me to a new way of seeing. In her the divisions of the past dissolved. The mistakes we sisters made together as a community were forgiven because she had discovered God in us and in herself. Despite the pain and sometimes insanity of the past, all that had endured was love.

"Sister," I said, "soon you will die and be with God. Someday I too will die. When from your life with God you see that I am dying, will you come to meet me, claiming my life for God?"

"Are you sure you want me to?"

"Yes, Sister, very sure."

"Then I will."

I knelt before her and asked her blessing. I felt her place her hand on my head and trace a tiny cross on my forehead. Then she rested her own head on top of mine and said softly,

"I will love you forever."

From her presence I arose to seek the expanse of the prairie. Alone I walked all the ancient paths into the woods and through the open fields of wheat and barley. Each tree and shrub greeted me, welcoming me home. I remembered a cliché of Mother Ann, the novice mistress: "Nothing is ever lost once we have seen; we always may be what we might have been," and smiled at the profundity of the simple. I no longer needed to discover my spirituality in opposition to the past.

Everything unfolds. Today carries all the joy and the pain, the triumphs and failures of yesterday, enfolding them, unfolding them, unfurling them into tomorrow. Marie Nativity is the birth mother of my soul, she is the ancient one, she is the womb of the womancircle out of which I came. I go forth with her wisdom in my heart, bearing her teaching into life. She made art of me. Nothing is ever lost. Here is Sophia and the Christ and they are one; earth and heaven and they are one; my past, my present and my every tomorrow and they are all one.

I stopped because I noticed a delicate sapphire insect with wings like transparent pearl—the small dragonfly they call a darning needle—poised atop the tallest spines of a stalk of barley. I watched, wondering why she did not fly away. Then I thought she must have died there. But she was so beautiful, beyond imagining, that I picked the stalk of barley thinking to carry it home with me. "Who are you, pearl-winged sister, and what is your meaning to me?" Just then I noticed that her fine legs were moving, still alive. Why didn't she fly? Examining her closely I discovered that she had been speared by four of the spines. They had not killed her, but they had imprisoned her securely. She must be free.

I was only vaguely aware of the hot sun, the sting of the deerflies, the prairie wind as I carefully removed three of the four spines. At last she had but one spine remaining in her heart. If I touched her to hold her while I pulled it loose, she would die, because my fingers could not be so delicate. So I reached as close as I could to the place where the spine entered her and, with my fingernails, I clipped it off as close to her body as I dared. Carrying the tiny spine still wedged into her heart she spread her wings of pearl, lifted herself upon the wind, and was free.

Circle 'Round the Cross

Blessed are the peacemakers,
they shall be called the children of
God.

EVERYDAY VIOLENCE

Where can peace begin? Here? Now? By what acts, what beliefs, what desires, what movements of the soul? Where is it lost to violent contradiction, where and why?

My neighbor across the street suffered the violence of World War II Austria. She keeps her silence. Keeps her peace? I think of the contradictions of every day, what might be called small violences compared to war, the maiming of the land, the nuclear threat, and the systematic elimination of the poor by ghetto-segregation and forgetfulness.

Years ago my father's plane crashed while he was on a Coast Guard rescue mission over Lake of the Woods. My mother wrote to me from my father's hospital room, where he was beginning to recover from reconstructive surgery on his face.

There is no doubt some plan for your father's future that does not include flying. This is just another added to the many close calls. I am grateful his life has been spared again. The plane carried *no* crash insurance but there will be a fair price for the salvage, I am sure. We just must forget about the flying end of the business and stay with the maintenance work only. No material profit in flying anyhow. For two weeks he made more money from trips than ever before—and in one minute's time, it was all washed out and more besides . . . I stayed with him all day Monday before surgery (after not shutting an eye all Sunday night) and after surgery. He had constant attention until 4:00 A.M. I slept from 11:30 to 3:30 and arrived at 4:00 A.M. to relieve the nurse who had done double duty—and I've been with him ever since.

I thank God for his life.

I held the letter tightly and walked up and down the block outside of Viterbo College trying not to cry, trying to regain some sense of peace. I felt slapped. To hear of his almost-death by letter, and almost a week after the event. To have been unable to be present to comfort my mother. To be unable, even then, to go to them or even call them by phone. I was a nun. My Superior declined my mother's request to contact me the night of the accident. "Your call will upset her. She has college exams this week. Wait."

I knew my father would begin to fly again the minute he was well enough. My mother would continue to suffer the violence of her fear. Their financial inability to insure the plane had led to even deeper indebtedness. He would be unable to work—there is no sick leave for the self-employed.

But mostly I felt violated by the unnatural restriction placed upon us. The contradiction felt overwhelming: They were my parents; I could not go to them; I could not go to them; I could not go.

What can we do about such contradictions to our well-being—such everyday violence? Its thrust is so small and its wound so deep. It is the response from a friend that never comes. It is the teasing word that sticks in the most fragile and secret fear of the heart. It is the irreconcilable disagreement with the one you most love. It is the resistance of your child to your help. It is being taken for granted. It is being caught in the tension between two people you love. It is the decision to construct a soul-wall against the rough retort. It is being ignored.

"It is not peace I have come to bring, but a sword," Jesus said (Matt. 10:34). What? Then later, "Peace I bequeath to you, my own peace I give you, a peace the world cannot give, this is my gift to you" (John 14:26–27). Contradictions?

What is this peace?

THE CROSS

Wait.

Watch for a moment. See the child in the street? See her carefully avoid the sidewalk cracks? See her teeter on one foot, leap, then tiny, tiny step across? So focused her intent. Would it really happen if she crossed the line, made a cross with her foot? Would she break her mother's back? A whisper in her mind says no. But you have to respect the magic. Be wary of your—perhaps—power. Just in case.

The mother must endure.

Wait.

A scream. Sound carries sharply, echoing off the hills. A crash, glass breaking. Where is this war? Which house? The man explodes, "Get into the car . . . *now*!" Again the woman's scream, with words this time, and sobs, "*No! No!* I'll *kill* you! Stop! *Stop!* I'll kill you. I won't go!" Then a child shrills, "Stop Mommy! Daddy, *stop! Please* . . ."

Terror. My terror—vibrations of sickening fear from the beating of their voices on the drum of my bodysoul. Can I do anything? Call the police? What if she means it? What if she kills me, or he kills her, or if both of them turn on the shrieking child?

Down the street the garage door on the sand-colored house opens automatically. A car careens backward into the street, shifts gears, screeches up the hill and around the corner. They are gone.

They are gone. The house is sold now. Another neighbor calls to say she received a letter from the woman who lived there—who hadn't said good-bye to anyone. "Tell the neighbors," she wrote, "we divorced. It was for the best; life was hell. I'm sorry I couldn't face you. I was so ashamed."

Wait.

"You disturb me," the woman's voice on the telephone is trembling. "What you say must be evil. Everything that disturbs must be evil, for doesn't scripture say that God comes not in the whirlwind. Unless you bring me peace I will not listen to you." I want to comfort her. I want to say there is no cross. I want to wrap her with wings. But the line between us is dead.

Wait.

What about the oak tree in the park. Torn. Spread open at the core. Back broken. Leaves.

Wait.

What happens here?

The Father falls from the sky.

The Mother is lost in the woods.

On a crisscross tree between earth and heaven a man who dreamed of peace has died.

The veil of the Temple is torn.

Wait.

> "Do not let your hearts be troubled or afraid.
> Peace I bequeath to you,
> my own peace I give you,
> a peace the world cannot give,
> this is my gift to you." (John 14:26, 27)

Wait.
What kind of Christ-crossed peace is this?

Wait.
We need some time to think. We need some time to pray.

CRISSCROSS, DOUBLE-CROSS

In the shadow of the cross I, like most Christians, have lived my life. Now, in these middle years, I ponder the effects of the cross's image on my personal history—my womanbody/womansoul. For every image we carry in our souls becomes physical, is lived out in our bodies. I love and fear this sign. In its power I have been created and destroyed; I have sold my soul and have been redeemed.

Before I could speak I could trace the sign of the cross upon my body.

From the time I could walk I toddled from Station to Station of the Cross during Lent. I held my mother's hand, knelt with her, stood with her, bowed my head, raised my eyes to the fourteen pictures as she told the crucifixion story—the story of Jesus "fixed to the cross" again and again. Over the years I walked this "Way of the Cross" thousands of times, allowing, even encouraging the imprint on my self of this powerful but inarticulate image.

For almost fifty years, and with an increasing sense of mystery, awe, and—lately—anger, I have watched the priest unveil the cross on the Friday we call "Good." I have listened to the chant, trying to understand with my heart what cannot be grasped by the mind.

> Behold the wood of the Cross,
> on which hung

the Savior of the world.
Come, let us adore.*

Lately I have wondered: What is the veil to mean that circles the tree of the cross? This solemn unveiling seems more fit an action for a bridal chamber than a place of violent death. Is there some mystic marriage here? Some *hieros gamos*? Some redeeming pain that is more of love than violence, but not without the violence, either; a pain that ends in peace and in a flowering of the very tree on which the man was torn and poured out?

> Faithful Cross, O tree all beauteous,
> Tree all peerless and divine:
> Not a grove on earth can show us
> Such a leaf and flower as thine.
> Sweet the nails and sweet the wood,
> Laden with so sweet a load.†

The grove of trees is the traditional temple of the Goddess. This grove created a womblike circle around the center tree, image of the god whom she contained, the god who was both her child and her lover. Is this circle 'round the cross, then, a sign of the wholeness of the Holy—Wisdom round the Christ—divine feminine and masculine oneness—Goddess reunited with the God? And is that reunion in our souls the source of peace and flowering? I don't know. He died. And the veil was torn.

One paradox we are facing here is pain. And the question is asked again by each generation—because it has no answer that can be passed forward from those who have lived it. Can pain be blessing? Is there any way to make peace with pain—as individuals or as a world? Do we dare make peace with a tree that has become a cross—a sign of contradiction? Can we accept being contradicted in all we believe personally, nationally, culturally, religiously? Can we be nailed to contradiction. Do we dare?

---

* The Solemn Veneration of the Cross: Roman Catholic Liturgy for Good Friday.

---

† "Crux Fidelis," a hymn by Fortunatus, Bishop of Poitiers, d. 609 C.E. Sung as part of the Roman Catholic Liturgy for Good Friday.

Or *must* we fight? Must we destroy the contra-diction, the contrary word, the other way, the otherness causing the pain that threatens our lives, our cherished selves? Or do those who make war on the Other, become, themselves, an Other? Peace begins only in the recognition that the Other is the shadow of our rejected selves. What we have rejected becomes the cross-beam on our world tree.

Can I continue to trace this sign upon myself? Can I say, "I am the cross; I will be the center tree and I will be the circling grove"?

> I am the contradiction
> I am the paradox
> I am where opposites meet
>   the four faces of the Divine
>   the four powers of the cosmos
>   the four directions of the world
>   the four elements of creation
>   On this Cross hangs the Savior . . .
>   the circle of the womb
>   the cycles of the moon
>   the spiral of cosmic creation
>   the grove of the Mother
>   Within this globe God is raised and the torn
>   tree flowers.
> "With Christ I am nailed to the cross
> And I live
> Now not I
> But Christ lives
> In me."
> I am the Circle.

THE CIRCLE

If we want peace we need to find it very close to home; we need to create it in the circle of our home, in our primary relationships. Some have suggested we could make peace within our own souls as a preliminary act to the promotion, on a grand scale, of world peace. But we do not proceed from isolated individual calm to peace between nations. There is no isolated peace. Isolation only silences the soul into a state that mystics call quietism. And there is no national or world peace among strangers unwilling to live through, with, and in the other. The Peace Movement is interpersonal; if not it becomes that ungrounded enthusiasm that mystics have traditionally called activism.

We make peace among us by a mutual act of indwelling. We do this with whomever is present. We do it within the circle of our personal lives, with whomever crosses our path within that circle. The circles widen until they circle the earth. Most often that widening is not our business. The present crossing is our business. This peace-making, here and now, with my friend, my spouse, my son, my sister, the clerk at Macy's, the child selling candy bars to buy uniforms for the PeeWee Soccer Team, the woman who writes in pain because her daughter has overdosed on cocaine, the nephew who needs a loan, the brother-in-law who is alone and sick, the candidate for local government who comes to the door seeking my vote, the hungry bag lady wandering through the produce market eating what she can pick up, the woman crying out in the house across the street.

We make peace where we can—where we are drawn to be. Peace in the home, peace in the corporation, peace at the ammunitions plant, peace in government, peace on the streets of the inner city, peace in the mountains, lakes, and forests, peace where whales are in danger of becoming extinct, peace in the churches, peace in the classrooms, peace where people are homeless.

I must confess to you that I don't do this well. I fear pain. I don't want to be hurt by the anger, or fear, or defensiveness, or hatred, or terror, or rejection of someone who crosses my path. I fear taking into that soft space of my self someone or some facet of creation whose own pain could tear at me until I become separated both within and between. I hesitate to circle the cross the two of us make, for the circle brings the other's pain into the sphere of my home.

The circles we draw define the limits of our selves and of our world. They include and exclude. Each of us can bear only so much contradiction at any given time in life. The circle will sometimes be quite small, sometimes large. Within the expanse of the circle, where opposites cross and reconcile, is the realm of peace. The blessing and promise of WomanChrist spirituality is that, finally, the circle will encompass the world.

When I was a child and cried over being rejected by a friend (a situation children seem to face almost daily) my mother taught me a little poem by Edwin Markham, called "Outwitted":

> He drew a circle that shut me out—
> Heretic, rebel, a thing to flout.
> But Love and I had the wit to win:
> We drew a circle that took him in.

Over the years I have needed to remember the wisdom of this rhyme many times. The child in me still draws the circle quite small, able to tolerate a minimum of the pain produced by contradiction and rejection. But now the woman I have become searches the depths for courage to make the circle of self ever more expansive, the home within ever more accepting. Since the beginning of time woman has made peace by circling.

> Woman is, herself, a circle.
> Circle of life's cycles, circle of the moon.
> Circle of womb around the cross of ovum and sperm.
> Circle of the primitive home, the global hut, designed
>   according to lines of earth, moon, and the cupped sky.
> Circle of the basket for gathering seed, for winnowing seed,
>   for sowing, harvesting, preserving.
> Circle of the bowl, the cup, the oven, the flask. Circle of
>   nourishment and life's continuing.
> Circle of the tribe, dancing the cosmic dance of creation,
>   developing language, making judgments.
> Circle of the Holy Being, belly round as the life-giving
>   earth, breasts held up and filled with milk, vulva
>   spread wide in birth-giving.
>
> And woman continues today.
> Circle of women opening to one another, encouraging each
>   woman's expression of her talents, telling each other
>   the truth, sharing food, home, and money with those
>   in need, speaking for one another in the marketplace,
>   educating one another.

Circle of shelter around women-victims of home violence.
Circle providing sanctuary to victimized children.
Circle of peace around military installations.
Circle of ritual and worship—in homes and on hillsides,
   by the ocean, in the mountains, in wooded groves, in
   church basements, on the streets at night.
Circles of creative power in boardrooms, at conference
   centers, at universities, at political caucuses: in
   Nairobi, Nicaragua, Cape Town, Saudi Arabia, Green-
   ham Commons, Washington, D.C.
Circles of dancing, circles of talk, circles of soulmaking,
   circles of judgment, circles of justice, circles of art,
   circles of childrearing, circles of prayer, circles of aid
   to those who need, circles of blessing all life—child in
   the womb, plant on the hillside, water in the aquifer,
   soaring hawk, migrating whale, the Amazon forests, the
   Nevada deserts, the air.

Woman is the circle grove around the tree of the cross. She makes peace by defining where we are at home; and eventually her circle will encompass the earth.

CIRCLE HOME

Family is the primal circle. Family initiates the most radical crossing we experience or ever will experience, because it is the focus for the deepest intimacy and indwelling. Family is the first home any of us knows, the cradle of love in which we learn the courage and generosity necessary for expansion of the circle throughout our lives. In the center of the family peace is made—or it is made nowhere.

Kathy and Steve sat across the table from me in the Good Earth restaurant on a cold October night in Minnesota. We cupped our hands around our steaming tea, enjoying the spicy aroma, glad to be out of the wind, glad to be together again after nearly a year, glad to anticipate our rising higher and higher on the tide of ideas and enthusiasm that always seemed to flow from our conversation.

"In spite of the Jungians' claim, individuation is *not* our ultimate goal." Steve's eyes twinkled with excitement, as was usual preceding the disclosure of one of his radical insights.

"The dyad is next." Kathy leaned forward, finishing Steve's thought. He smiled as if he had said it himself. Both of them focused their gaze on me so that the energy of it met and combined somewhere just before entering me. One gaze.

"Two individuated persons forming a dyad," Steve again. "And then, maybe, community. But we are nowhere near that yet. It *is* the progression, though."

"Kathy is with me always—not only when we are in each other's physical presence, but when I am at the office trying to solve a technical problem, or hiking alone in the woods, or commuting to a meeting in Atlanta. She is the *life* of it all. My home.

"If Kathy were to die, I would go on living, certainly. But I think that something would be gone out of everything. Something in the air, in the trees, in the lakes and mountains that is there now because of her. Or maybe *I* would be gone somewhere else with her spirit and would be only physically here in this world."

"But we have come to believe this oneness we have with each other is something else than dependence." Kathy smiled peacefully, warmly. "We've been married nearly twenty years. Our friends used to laugh at us when we worried that we might be dependent on each other. They seemed to think that dependence would paralyze a relationship long before twenty years had elapsed. Our experience is something else. Growth. Not absence of pain and struggle. But constant, beautiful growth."

The waitress came with our meals. We discontinued our conversation momentarily to chat with her, comment on our choices for food, pour wine and toast our friendship, and offer thanks for the grace of God's blessing in earth's fruits. In another part of my mind I mused over these two people, my friends, a man and woman who seemed to love each other more than anyone else I had ever met. Their love communicated itself to so many others in an unself-conscious generosity. I wasn't sure that Steve and Kathy were even aware of how thoroughly they had become a blessing in the lives of so many others.

A memory flickered. I lay sick on their living room sofa. I had lost my job, had no money for housing, and was alone.

"You can live here 'til you find something. It's no problem. There's an extra bed and plenty of food." They opened their lives and I came in. I lived in their home for a month before I found another job and an apartment of my own. I never left their lives.

"Um, good wine," Kathy murmured. I was brought back to the Good Earth and our conversation. "Tell Christin what Savary said."

"Oh, yes." Ordinarily Kathy's role was to pose questions, Steve's to speculate on them. "This was at a conference on couple's spirituality. You know this priest, Louis Savary? Well, he was the speaker, and had some good things to say. Anyway, he had this stunning insight about the Eucharistic prayer and the marriage relationship. You know where the priest says, just before the Great Amen, 'Through Him and with Him, and in Him are given to You, Oh Holy God, in the unity of the Holy Spirit, all honor and glory forever'? Well, it is the *through, with,* and *in* that are the essence of the communion of love. It is the way Christ is in communion with us by our communion with each other.

"We open the center of ourselves and receive the other one. It's a communion of being, a transcendence of individuality, a beginning of participation—and maybe more than a beginning—in everything, in God."

Steve brought us back to the Eucharist. "So, that is what Jesus meant: *"You in me and I in them, that we all may be perfectly one'* (John 17:22, paraphrase by Steve). Anyway, *through him* is physical oneness; *with him* is oneness of psyche or soul, and *in him* is the oneness that is of the spirit."

Kathy beamed. "So you see the implications for marriage? For making a home?"

"Finding the center, opening the center, allowing another 'center' to enter and meld into oneness—both increasing individuation and transcending it, becoming this openness physically, psychically, spiritually. That's what marriage is all about. That was what Jesus was all about."

And peace, I thought. This communion is the origin of peace and creates the circle of their home.

From 1974 until 1982 I spent my life with children whose families had broken and dropped them outside the circle of the home. We came together in a children's shelter and residential treatment center in Minneapolis; it was a place called a "home"—St. Joseph's Home for Children. I was their chaplain. In 1983 I told our story, theirs and mine, in *Caring Community: A Design for Ministry.**

These children taught me the results of broken circles, of what people become to themselves and others when they are truly homeless. Loss of roots, hope, power, and meaning characterize their restless lives. I can see these children in my mind's eye still: Sara curled into a fetal position on my office floor, pleading, "Don't love me, please don't love me, it will hurt too much . . . unless, if you would be my mother, maybe then it would be all right."

Joyce throwing my books against the wall, climbing up on my desk, crouching like a cornered cat, glaring, screaming, "You think you're *God!* Well, you're wrong. There is no God! All there is is *hate!* And you are too. You are *hate!* I hate you, I hate you, I hate you. Let me go! Let me die!"

Kevin sitting alone on the concrete step outside the door to my office, staring out past the apple orchard, toward the skyline of the city. When I asked what he was doing, he replied, "I was just thinking . . . Out there somewhere must be a family who would accept a boy like me. There must be a home for someone who wants one so much."

I see the child flailing like a captured animal, screaming obscenities at the counselors who are attempting to hold him, to keep him from injury. I see the child running down the hall, through the unlocked doors, down the long walk to the waiting car of a pimp or drug dealer promising "protection" in a pseudo-home. I see the child returning sick from drugs, or raped and crying, filled with guilt for being victim of a crime.

Again I read my "Letter to the Children," written at a time when they surrounded me with their pain and longing for a home that would last.

You are not broken things which we can mend with glue. You yourselves have said it: It is your hearts that are broken. You require our love as well as our skill. You require our care for each other as a sign that love and its healing power are possible. You dream of us joining our lives around you

---

* Christin Lore-Kelly, *Caring Community: A Design for Ministry* (Chicago: Loyola University Press, 1983).

and creating a human cradle—a new home in which you can have the security to be healed and to grow. We must be committed to each other for you.*

Most often we were—parents with social workers with pastoral ministers with educators with psychologists. Most often we succeeded in mending broken circles or creating circles where none had existed before. Most often when a child graduated from St. Joseph's Home some peace had been made around that child's life; and "home" had become possible again.

When we focused ourselves on the children peace became possible. They are the peacemakers because of their weakness and vulnerability. They cry out to what is most sensitive in us, most soft, most creative. They want to come in. When we won't let them in, or when we won't come out to them they scream with fear and anger because their very being is threatened. They try to hurt us to get our attention. Their restlessness is the outward manifestation of our lack of peace.

The children saw through pretence. They knew when they were loved; they tested the love where they saw it in order to feel whether or not it would last. They knew when they were simply a goal we needed to achieve or a task we needed to perform. They resisted us then. They responded when they sensed that we were sincere—that our "doing" was our "being made active."

Peace is made and home is created when we pay attention to what is weak or most fragile in us—ourselves, our loved ones, the peoples, nations, lands, animals, and earth of this world. When we honor that weakness and circle it with our love and care, we proclaim that being itself is sacred. We proclaim that every facet of creation is connected and flows through, with, and in every other facet.

What is weak is never separate from me, but is essential to my continued being. Caring for what is fragile in this world and in ourselves teaches us the true quality of our strength. In our response to fragility and weakness we learn whether or not our power is suffused with enough wisdom to bring forth peace.

The fragility of the world, wherever it is found—in the child, the poor, the oppressed, in the secret places of each of our hearts—

---

* *Ibid.,* "Letter to the Children."

requires of us a fullness of being and a surrounding with care. Fragility focuses our attention on creation: For if we do not nourish what is fragile it will die and take what is holy in us with it.

Home is acceptance. We are at home when we are both known intimately and accepted fully, and when what is most fragile in us is most carefully served. We create home when we so serve others in this world. Our deepest instinct calls us to find and create wider and more inclusive homes until nothing is excluded from the circle. Circling and centering the all-inclusive home is what we call God—the most peaceful and most fragile of all.

BLESSED ARE THE PEACEMAKERS

Suffer us not to mock ourselves with falsehood
Teach us to care and not to care
Teach us to sit still
Even among these rocks,
Our peace in His will
And even among these rocks
Sister, mother
And spirit of the river, spirit of the sea,
Suffer me not to be separated

And let my cry come unto Thee.

T. S. ELIOT, "Ash Wednesday"*

This is the work of peace: truth, detachment, trust, wisdom, and awe. The work of peace directly opposes the forces of destruction in our world: lies, possessiveness, control, dualism, and egocentricity.

---

* "Ash Wednesday," T. S. Eliot, *Selected Poems* Part VI (New York: Harcourt, Brace & World, 1964), 93.

TRUTH

"Suffer us not to mock ourselves with falsehood"

Here it begins. Truth grounds peace, is the earth from which it springs, in our hearts and between our hearts wherever we meet—in our homes, our neighborhoods, our cities, our nations. Here is a paradox. Peacemaking requires struggle. We struggle to see the truth, to know the truth, to tell the truth, to be the truth. If we do not listen carefully enough we kill the truth and our peace with it.

"I came into the world for this: to bear witness to the truth; and all that are on the side of truth listen to my voice." Such was the only defense of Jesus. The governor's response? "Truth? What is that?" And killed him (John 18:37–38).

We cannot make peace by covert strategy, trickery, or "disinformation." The best result possible from such efforts is stalemate. Even what we call "détente" is simply a mutual agreement to "relax" from the struggle. Détente means a loosening, a letting go. It is not peace. It is often a decision to live for a time in our own falsehood, letting our lies rest, letting the others go to their own falsehoods.

We get tired. We decide to rest from either war or the struggle for peace. We do this within ourselves and between. Such détente is refusal of the dyad relationship, that "inscaping" by which we experience the truth of self and other simultaneously. We agree on separation. We do this in our marriages, our families, our nations, our world.

The feminine and masculine modes of our being complement one another in the search for truth. The masculine seeks truth directly by sorting out experience, differentiating, categorizing, and prioritizing. Truth is considered to be the most logical interpretation resulting from this process. Its characteristic is clarity. The feminine, on the other hand, circles experience, compounds its various elements into multidimensionality. Truth is considered to be present in the most complex pattern. Its characteristic is paradox.

"I'm confused and despondent." It was Janice on the phone, calling from the Midwest. I could feel in her voice that characteristic restrained intensity. I allowed an image of her to form within me—small, energy tightly packed in a wiry body, darting green eyes under thick lashes, ruddy skin, wispy red hair cut short for convenience. I saw her both as she was later, in soft corals and sea greens and gold; and as I first encountered her—in scruffy jeans, confronting me with a challenge and rebellious stance. I listened.

"I've been working with a spiritual director from the Cenacle—not too successfully—thinking perhaps I could use her as a supervisor in my internship. I need an institution where I can intern—I expect my advisor at the college to present me with an ultimatum very soon. 'Go to the Cenacle, or to Loyola Center, or to the Benedictine Center; but *go* somewhere!'

"Anyway, she threw up her hands the other day and said, 'I don't know what we are doing here—whatever it is it isn't the Ignatian Exercises!'

"The Exercises did keep me praying, I have to say that for them. Other than that, I couldn't follow them—they seem so sin-centered. And the thought process in them is so masculine.

"So what am I supposed to do? I don't seem to fit into any system. I just don't know who or what I am . . . *where* I fit. What can I do? I've spent all this time in school; at mid-life, yet. And now I don't know if I fit anywhere, if I can make use of my education and training anywhere in the institution of the church.

"I keep trying to get at the truth. What am I? What am I supposed to do with my life? What is my *meaning* here? There are so many options. Which one fits me? How can I know what to do if I can't figure out who I am? You'd think that after forty years I would know who I am! But I'm like a moon that keeps changing—not just in shape, but in its place in the sky. So what is the truth about me and about my life?

"Jack says I make it all too complicated. For him everything seems so easy. He figures out what to do and he does it. Then the only thing that *is,* is what is there. Do you know what I mean? He can somehow limit himself to just the simple present. I envy him a little—but I also don't think I could be like that. It feels unreal—like you tell a lie to yourself by not seeing the total picture. But when I see the whole picture, I get so confused!"

We need both energies, balanced, to live in truth. For truth is a way of being before it is an expression of being. "I *am* the truth," says Jesus. Truth is never fixed; it is constantly expanding as we evolve in the cosmic creative process. All that I am today is only a part of what I will be tomorrow, and the same can be said of all my relationships and of the relationships that constitute all of reality.

Peacemaking is rooted in the struggle for truth. Think close to home. Think about conflict with someone you love. How does it feel? For me conflict ordinarily results from some basic misunderstanding. I become afraid. I want to run away. What if I can't find the words to tell the truth of what I am right now; why I have done what I have done? What if I *can* tell the truth and he will not accept me because of it? I stumble and choke on my attempts. I often cry. It is so hard; which words will work? I look at him, I try to find the softness in him—the place I can enter even if I am clumsy. It can take hours; can we endure the strain? We attempt. "No, no I didn't mean that; I meant . . ." "I don't *know* why I do it, I don't understand that part of me, I want to understand; I don't want to hurt you." I can barely breathe. We each see the pain. We hold each other for reassurance. Then we begin again. It does take hours. We finally understand and live through, with and in each other again. For the moment we have our truth—and peace.

On a national level we have "summit meetings," when what we need are meetings deep in the ground of our common earth. We cannot keep peace by defending ourselves against the other's truth or refusing to listen to our common needs. Where we have contradiction we must work toward paradox. While the process of creation continues, truth weaves itself into ever more complex patterns, which fall apart over and over again, which transform into greater complexity. This is the nature of the cosmos. This is our nature. We must accept this, and in our acceptance is our peace.

DETACHMENT

"Teach us to care and not to care"

I just returned from the shopping mall, a place I can tolerate for only brief periods at those times when I need to purchase a product I can find nowhere else. I hate to shop. Nevertheless, each time necessity forces me into the marketplace, I am impressed by how much in the minority I am. People, mostly women and girls, appear to be totally engrossed in the task, taken up, invigorated by it.

Some, enlivened by their purchasing goals, move through the mall with a deliberation that is exhausting to witness. Nothing stands in their way—not price, nor rarity, nor the aching feet that result from the search through seemingly endless rows of shops. Nothing daunts their resolve. They will return home with the prize, exalting.

Others are playful. Often in groups of two or more they move with ease, almost in a dance motion, through the maze of products. It is a carnival, a dreamland, where wishes come true. The playful ones try on clothes like children playing dress-up, twirl before mirrors, douse themselves with expensive cologne samples, sit at the Estée Lauder counter for make-up demonstrations—and they buy. They buy and they buy. Once I saw a bumper sticker that read "I live to shop!"

Finally there are a few shoppers like me. Just the attempt to find a parking place is enough to deter us. Opening the door and entering the throng saps at least half our strength. You can recognize us by our slumped shoulders and dejected expressions.

If the needed product is not in the first store, where we expect it to be, we experience momentary panic. We reach deep into our reserves of energy and set about the search. Five or six stores constitute a limit. Finally we find it. By this time, though, our minds are fuzzy—do I really need it? Does it cost too much? It isn't quite right, but will it do? We are poised on a very keen edge here. Sometimes we grit our teeth, grab hold, and buy the thing. Sometimes we put it back, unable to endure another moment's strain. Sometimes we pick it up, carry it to the checkout counter, and wait in line. A breath could change our minds now. I have often changed my mind at the last moment, dropped the product on the first table I see, and fled the store.

At home John asks how it went. "I failed," I admit with frustration, "failed at shopping again!"

Shopping raises some deep questions for me: What is valuable? What gives life? What can be possessed? To what am I connected?

Of what can I let go? How much or little do I need? Where do I invest my care?

Shopping in this context is a metaphor for the drive toward possession. And in a materialistic society the more I possess, the more of a person I am. This notion would be incomprehensible to many peoples in the history of the world. The Pacific Coast Indians, for example, measured greatness not by how much a person owned, but by how much a person could give away as gift.

"The man who dies with the most toys, wins!" reads another bumper sticker. Wins what? A friend and I used to browse in art galleries and antique stores. She would pause before a particularly beautiful piece and murmur, "Ummm, I love this piece, exquisite line, subtle color. The pleasure of looking at it is marvelous." But she never bought anything. Once I asked her why, with the intensity of her appreciation, she had not acquired much art for her own possession.

"Oh," she laughed, "I discovered long ago that I do not need to *own* something to derive pleasure from it. In fact I already own more than enough for a lifetime—I can hardly care for it all. No. Rather than buy these beautiful things I prefer to admire them where they are, implant the image firmly in my soul, and live with it for as long as I remember. It feels to me as though I am part of all the beautiful things in the world and that everything I see has become a part of me. I don't need to own them. Also," she grinned mischievously, "I don't need to dust them."

What emptiness do we seek to fill with the quantities of things we buy? Or are we trying to hold ourselves down with possessions because we have found nothing in our lives real enough to receive and nourish the roots of our souls? No amount of things, regardless of their worth or beauty, will ever be enough. The more we seek to possess the more dissatisfied we will become. The way to fullness of life is the way of dispossession.

Without attachment to life we cannot detach ourselves from the trivialities we seek to possess. But the reality is that we never possess life, we participate in it. We send down roots into the vast ground of being. Peace wells up from the depths into which we have plunged our most intensely committed care.

Care rooted in our deepest realities provides us the security to let go of the unneeded trivialities. We simply do not care for them anymore. They do not satisfy. They bring no peace.

TRUST

"Teach us to sit still
Even among these rocks,
Our peace in His will"

We are not in control. When Pat lay dying he announced to his gathered friends, "I am going to God now." But he didn't die that day. The next day and the next, people came to bid him farewell. Many spoke to him although he was no longer conscious; many told him it was all right to go to God. Finally P.J. leaned over my chair and whispered to me, "I don't think we are the ones in control here."

Even in tragic circumstances we can be struck with amusement at the absurd caricature we humans make of ourselves when we play God. So, despite the inexorable approach of my husband's death, I began to let myself live in the present as it was. I relaxed. I ate a bit of fruit. I listened to Pachelbel's "Canon in D" hoping that Pat could hear it too, on the other side of consciousness.

My mind played a few tricks on me. I remember thinking, "Well, if this hospice room is where we are going to live for the rest of our lives, we might as well make a home of it." I settled in for what seemed forever. Not that it seemed of long duration, it seemed eternal. Now I think I was suspended, floating, held by the Will of the Holy One. I do not remember having a will of my own. I simply lived each moment.

For three days and three nights I had not slept. Perhaps I thought that if I remained watching he would not die. Now, in this new "home" of ours, allowing myself to join him in sleep seemed natural. I lay my hand on his and closed my eyes. And Pat died.

The Will of God is not controlling, not judgmental, not a secret I need to ferret out, not stringent, not against my nature. It is not a blueprint for life nor a road map to heaven. It is what is deepest in me.

When I was young I was told to strive for perfection. I thought the admonition meant always to do more than I could and be more than

I was. As a result I became always anxious about what I was supposed to be doing. The anxiety made my head ache. I also became guilty about never measuring up. The guilt made my stomach hurt. Wouldn't it be grand, I thought, if I could just be myself?

"Teach us to sit still." We need rest. We need to stop our anxious striving long enough to feel who we are. We need to feel the beauty of ourselves, the power of ourselves, the intricate wholeness of ourselves. We need to trust the wisdom by which we are designed. Controlling ourselves to fit into some rationalized notion we might have or might have been told is "God's will" is futile and a mistake. God's will is never imposed.

Sitting still sometimes means resistance. We sit still against all that threatens the ongoing life of this planet: poison and war and exploitation of creatures and lands. We sit still against those who would judge us by rules that contain nothing of women's wisdom. We sit still against taunts, trivializations, and attempts of the vengeful to victimize us; we refuse to participate. We sit still when all that is most essential to our womanselves cries out in protest. Our sitting is protest. Our protest is the Will of God—our peace and our peacemaking.

"Even among these rocks," wherever we are. If mothers, we make peace in mothering. If artists, we make peace by our art. If farmers, we make peace by growing food. To what are you drawn by your deepest desire? Let yourself be drawn; it is the Will of God.

P.J. and I sat by the pool in the California sunshine. "I put all this time into dancing," she mused, "but what does it accomplish? Does it bring peace? Should I be demonstrating at the Concord Naval Weapons Station instead? Which way of using my time and energies would contribute most to peace?"

If you are a dancer, dance.
If you are a poet, write a poem.
If you are a wanderer, walk the countries of the earth.
If you are a listener, hear the stories of the people.
If you love music, sing.
If you are moved by people's pain, become a healer.
If the cries of the hungry echo in your heart, feed them.
If your soul requires solitude, go to the woods and care for the trees.
If you are a leader, lead.

If you are thirsty for knowledge, seek after Wisdom and drink from Her Cup.

It is the Will of God.

WISDOM

"Suffer me not to be separated"

John woke me as I cried "no."

"It's all right. It was only a dream." He cradled me into the hollow of his body and surrendered once again to his own sleep.

Only a dream. The question again: Do what are only dreams become in time what only is real? What remained of this night's dream? Snatches. Four women held me. They were going to kill me, drown me. They were garbed—priestesses? shamans? The black-garbed woman sentenced me to death. Why? What did I do? "You tried to combine fire and water. For this you must die." I struggled for release. I screamed. John woke me as I cried *"No!"*

P.J. brought out the costumes for the spider woman dance and the mermaid dance. "The two images came to me together," she explained, "and the only way to live creatively and wholly is to balance the energy of the two. They can never be separated or they will destroy us."

Fire and water, spider woman and mermaid woman, Kali and Aphrodite, death and birth, violence and bliss. . . . "I had this dream . . ." I said, and shared it with her.

"Did you know," P.J. interjected excitedly into my story, "that Stone Age clan women are believed to have carried fire in their vaginas? They wrapped the coals that were necessary to the life of the clan and carried them inside, next to their wombs, in that place of moist life. They were the firebearers. They knew the balance of fire and water, how to combine them. They had to know or die." Her eyes shone. "If that were my dream I would interpret it as a sign that I am a firebearer."

"But they were trying to *kill* me, P.J. Why would *women* be trying to kill me?"

"*Who* were they trying to kill?" Piercingly. Meaningfully.

Of course: the image I had of myself. My ego-self. The identity devised for others to see. The identity meant to protect all that was most vulnerable.

"Four is the sign of wholeness."

"Yes, the four women represent my whole self, the conjunction of all opposites, the image in me of Wisdom."

"Aren't you writing about the reconciliation of opposites?" P.J. was really excited now.

"Yes, but that was why I couldn't understand. Why should I be killed for trying to reconcile the opposites?"

P.J. smiled. "It's *your* dream."

"I know! It is because I am *trying*. The reconciliation cannot happen at that level, at the level of the ego *trying*. That is too manipulative. I must be drowned. I must descend into the depths, deeper than reason, deeper than trying. Wisdom reconciles. Or, rather, in Wisdom what we see as opposites have never been separated."

We must drown in her. "Sister, Mother, and spirit of the river, spirit of the sea." The work we do for peace is first of all an acceptance of the Wisdom within each of us who runs deeper than our surface separations or dualisms. Peace is a quality of being before it is a work of combining the fire and water of the world. We cannot simply decide, as if we had the power at the disposal of our egos, to make peace. The source of peace is Wisdom. And we are called to drown into Her depths.

She bears fire in her watery womb.

AWE

"And let my cry come unto Thee."

We made a circle at twilight on Holy Thursday. Outside the full moon of Passover glowed silver against dusky rose and violet. We made a circle in a chapel made of stone. We lit candles to set in the windows against the descending dark. We made a circle with the Poor Clare nuns, we made the circle in their home, their worship place, their bridal chamber, their place of truth and peace. We made a circle of ourselves—we who were women, men, and children, homemakers and guests in this stone place. Around an open, empty space we circled, waiting in silence. Even the children sat motionless, holding breath, wondering.

Almost inaudible, the sounding of a bell. Tiny Krista reached up with her arms; we were standing now. I lifted her to the sight of the procession of women in long brown robes, women with incense, women bearing a simple cross, women with banners and bells, coming into the center, leading the priest to the center, bringing the cross to the center. Krista whispered, "God is coming!"

She listened to the reading of the story as though she were old enough to understand. She heard how Jesus took a pitcher of water and a towel and prepared to wash the feet of his friends. She watched as the nuns prepared the water and bowls for the memorial. She saw the first of the sisters remove their sandals. One of the nuns passed solemnly in front of us.

Krista whispered, "I want to see."

"We are accustomed to children," Sister Bernadette had told us before the celebration began, "let them feel at home." I whispered back to Krista, "Go and see. It will be all right."

Krista glanced back once for confidence and then tiptoed lightly into the center. Tiny creature there in the emptiness. Alone but unafraid, she approached the footwashing.

Krista knelt before the priest. Krista took a pitcher of water and poured it over his feet; she took a towel and dried them gently, carefully. Then she went from person to person with the towels, smiling, unself-conscious with joy.

When all the adults had been served Krista whispered to Sister Bernadette, "I want to feel the water." She reached her little hand into the pitcher. "It's warm," she smiled. "Will you wash my feet?"

The child in the center pulled off her shoes and socks as children do. She extended her little feet for the pouring of the water and the nun washed the feet of the child.

When it was completed Krista came back through the center. She seemed bathed in sunlight. We watched her, the rest of us, our eyes shining near tears. She was our golden child, belonging to us all. In her innocence we transcended our limited egos, our shame, our reluctance to serve and be served, our grasping for power.

She climbed onto my lap. "She washed my feet," Krista whispered with delight.

When we are centered in our own egos we are limited from that gift of peace of which Jesus spoke at his last Passover: "Peace I bequeath to you, my own peace I give to you, a peace the world cannot give, this is my gift to you" (John 14:26).

Such peace springs as easily as the laughter of a child from awe-filled hearts. For awe is the child of our own innocence—and each of us contains that golden quality, despite those experiences of our lives that seem to have denied it, hidden it, smeared it with shame. The innocence remains, shines, somewhere in the center of the circle of self, somewhere in the empty spaces.

Awe finds so much joy in seeing that she forgets her shame at being seen. Awe kneels before the mighty in the innocent belief that a little water can wash away fear and reveal and nourish love. Awe is not solemn; it is playful and light of heart. And in the soul of Awe a cry resounds always, in all places, of all things: "God is coming."

CENTER PEACE

Here I am tenderest, softest. Here, where I am most whole, I can be most easily torn. Here the center of who and what I am will now be open. Come in. What I have protected fearfully I now expose as the essence of me. Come in. What is soft in me and open to you becomes strong when we mingle. I cross my weakness with your strength, my intensity with your calm, my courage with your fear, my doubt with your belief. When we have come over into each other, then we cannot be overcome. We have dared the paradoxical violence of making peace.

We are water and fire, earth and air. We cross. We are the elements of being, the compass points of Holy Wisdom, who reaches from end to end mightily and orders creation with sweetness. Why do we fear the cross when She is the circle round us?

We say our enemy destroys our peace, so we must conquer the enemy. Is the enemy, then, a monster incarnated by the intensity and isolating protectiveness of our fear? Fear is the mother of Defense. Defense brings forth Blame. Blame breeds Conflict and the assumption of Power. When I take power over another I alienate the other, create an enemy, and declare a state of war.

So come through the earth of me, with the soul of me, in the spirit transcending me. Enter the softness and of our daring, make peace. This is the healing, the returning to wholeness, the centerpeace. More than bringing together the separated—the torn—making peace brings the other *in. With and in.* Peace is born from the center, as a result of the interchange, crossing through earth, with soul, in spirit. Contradiction becomes a Word on the Cross, where opposites meet and meld. All is encircled by Wisdom, the Sister-Mother who is Spirit of the river and of the sea, who is creation's Divine Soul.

THE EIGHTH BLESSING

Visions and Tears

*Blessed are those who are pesecuted
for justice's sake,
theirs is the fullness of heaven.*

SEERS

We've come round the year to April. Alone in the afternoon sunlight I climb the hill to the torn oak. There where the new green struggles to survive I leave my offerings—a small white shell, a smooth black stone, a blood-red rose, and a song upon the wind.

I know I stand at an edge, a keen precipice of faith to which the meditation and the prayer of this writing has brought me. And I can neither step out nor stand here very long. Here I am permeable to the wind, as transparent as light. I can be seen only by those who share the precipice. I am blind.

As the Lady Justice is blind. As Tiresias is blind. Blind in the serving of seeing.

This torn oak tree is a threshold. Beyond it could be nowhere, could be chaos, could be the moment before creation when being remained a question in the heart of God, remained a vastness in Wisdom's Cosmic Womb. We have not seen it yet, what *could* be were we not so torn, were we to step through that torn place in creation into the core where what is new has, perhaps, taken root. Even the Seers have not seen.

They have not dared.

My song falls silent before I am finished. I find I have forgotten the words. As an unseasonable rain gusts in from the Pacific, I become aware of my own tears. I leave the shell, the stone, and the rose where the oak is torn. I turn my face to the wind.

"I don't know if I can continue," I tell John. I am not looking at him. We are in bed, lying against the pillows, both staring at some undetermined point on the wall, both focusing intently within.

"What do you mean?"

"I mean, if I continue with this work of reconciling opposites will I end up losing everything? Can you go out too far searching for truth? I have tried to be faithful to the search believing I was responding to some kind of Call into a deeper and deeper Reality. But perhaps by being faithful I have lost my faith."

"Of course you have," John smiles. "You *have* lost your faith over and over again each time a broader and more inclusive reality has become visible to you. You could have stopped, you know. I think a lot of people do; they stop with a particular view of the world and of God, a particular set of beliefs and morals and they say to themselves, 'This feels comfortable to me, I can live with this for the rest of my life.' And they do. They are faithful to that. It answers their questions—most of them anyway. The questions it doesn't answer, they simply stop asking."

"I couldn't do that," I frown.

"I know." John turns to me. He is grinning. He kisses me on the nose. "I've accepted that about you, why can't you accept it? Remember the poem you read to me some time ago? The one about the seers? Who was the poet?"

"Denise Levertov."

"Right. Get it out and read it again. We need to hear it."

I reach into the wicker book basket at the side of the bed and come up with *Oblique Prayers*.

"Read it aloud." John leans back.

SEERS

> They make mistakes:
> they busy themselves,
> anxious to see more, straining their necks to look
> beyond blue trees at dusk,
> forgetting it is
> the dust at their feet reveals
> the strangest, most needful truth.
> They think they want
> a cherishing love to protect them
> from the anguish they must distribute, the way
>   wives of cruel kings handed
>   loaves of bread to the poor—
> a love that delights in them: but when
>
> ironic Time gives them such love
> they discover—and only then—its weight, which,
> if they received and kept it, would crush down
> the power entrusted to them.
> The tender lover,

> aghast at what he sees them seeing, or blind
> and gently denying it, would set
> a wall of lead about them,
> hold down their feathered
> Hermes-feet,
> close the eyes that brim
> not with tears but with visions,
> silence the savage music
> such golden mouths
>   are sworn to utter.*

I closed the book. Seers. All of us women are seers today. Our faith is in our commitment to seeing. Even standing at the edge of all that we have ever known, all that we have ever loved. Even when the other side is darkness.

"I never want you to close your eyes," John whispers.

"Despite the tears?"

"Because of the visions."

VISIONS

I speak for myself here. In other places I tell the stories of others, wonder about them, offer my interpretations. But here I speak for myself. The others have their own words, their own visions.

When I was a girl I went off to find God. I went where God was rumored to be: the convent. What did I know of nuns? Only what I read in stories of the saints, only what I felt from my piano teacher thirty minutes twice a month, only what I saw from a distance. I didn't go there because of them. I went to find God.

And I did.

I found God in the women, and in the land.

---

* Denise Levertov, *Oblique Prayers* (New York: New Directions, 1984), 11.

I called God "Christ," and worshiped him in everything. In my journal I wrote:

To the Paschal Christ:

You catch me unaware in the brilliant red of a leaf caught under ice in a springtime pool hidden by a wooded path, in smooth thorn's red berries shining against snow, in delicate miniature leaves of April. You are the Mystery in the unsought. Your power explodes in a cascading river ice-break on a Holy Thursday afternoon; Your beauty sparkles through tree limbs in a fairyland of frost infused with the roselight of morning. You cannot be killed in my dying. Even when I do not look for You, You do not escape notice. My eyes are caught, held, by your Body in the leaf, the thorn, the frost; and my spirit is transformed through Your Body returned to life.

To the Christ-Spirit:

You are the wide sky of the prairie. To You my heart homes and into You my dreams expand. When nothingness grips my soul, wringing it dry, You rain grace. You wrap me in breezes and I sing. Your Spirit is the sky and Your Song fills the wind. We sing together in ecstatic harmony that winds around the arches of the world. When I walk the vastness of your Soul, You show me stairs formed of light and space and beckon me beyond. I float upon the air to the pinnacle where I am veiled in moonlight and as Your melody crescendos I am dancing—dancing.

To the Earth-Christ:

Your paths wind labyrinthine within a magic circle into the mystic woods. Sunlight filters through leaves of maple, elm, and oak to caress with warmth the delicate Ladyslipper among the ferns. Now singing, now silent women wend their way spiraling to the forest's heart to the place of the five trees—ancient, mothers of the entire woods. Beneath their thick branches the forest floor is clean. The women who have named the trees, who are intimate with them, dance in the thin green light. Then resting, one woman cradled on a low branch, another swinging in a circle of vine, others leaning against substantial tree trunks, they begin to tell the beads. Their voices murmur a cadence of women's mysteries praising the Great Mother with rhythm like a lullaby—"Blessed are you, and blessed is the fruit of your womb." Earth absorbs the blessing while wind wafts its music toward the Sun.

To Christ of the Waters:

Your water perfectly reflects the sky at dusk: orange, rose, and burgundy light intense upon stillness. The wild blue heron poises, one foot raised to hiddenness, statuesque but alive more than if she moved. Breaking the water, a northern pike splashes and sends circles radiating endlessly, shifting the face of the sky, combining the colors. You are mist drifting in at twilight, lifting at dawn. We take the boat just before the sun rises and push away from shore to be lost in You, one with Your Silence. The first bird sings to greet the sun and our voices, too, rise to welcome the morning:

> My heart is steadfast, O God;
> My heart is steadfast;
>   I will sing and chant praise.
> Awake, O my soul; awake lyre and harp!
>   I will wake the dawn. . . .
> Be exalted in the heavens, O God;
>   In all the earth be your glory (Ps. 56)

To Christ of Solitude:

You are emptiness at midnight and no one beside me at dawn; cool starkness holding me so that I do not cry aloud: "I am not dead, I am not no one, there is a world within me here, covered by this veil." You are one winter tree standing against the snow-swept horizon cradling a full moon in naked branches. You are the tracks of one deer across a frozen field. You are one golden leaf riding the autumn wind. You are wandering the lonely roads of all the world. You are old and young, poor and rich, woman and man—You are the abandoned of God. O Christ, O Shekinah, O Wisdom, O Silenced One, I have met You on the road and I have walked with You. I reach my hands to touch your face—O Ancient-Ever-Young—and touch the moon. I am naked branches leaning against the night, outcast upon Your Silence.

This Christ I came to know was the same as the one whom Paul called the Sophia of God. The One within and containing all our images, all our visions. This Christ is not nor ever has been limited to either earth or sky, feminine or masculine, silence or word. This is the Christ of our connectedness who wraps all our many gods and goddesses in an embrace of compassionate wholeness.

This was the one I went to the convent to find. I am not sure who I found. I remember a little prayer that I read on a holy card and which accompanied my search:

> Lord, I do not know
> As for so long I have not known,
> If love of Thee or me
> Now reaches out my hands.
> Let it be Thee.

Whoever it was who came to me as God, in the earth and sky, in the women with whom I lived, in prayer, in the Gospels, in the liturgical mysteries—that One I loved. That One I called the Christ. That One called me, too, by name.

Since convent days I have passed through many thresholds of faith in my search for God. A few things I have learned. To listen to the Voice of the Holy One. To follow where the Voice leads. Not to be surprised at the unorthodoxy of God. Never to deny my vision. Never to silence my voice.

In the darkness at each successive threshold of faith, when tears well up for all that will be lost as I pass through, there is One who remains. One who holds me even as I let go of all I thought I knew. It is the Christ. Christ, the depth of the Wisdom of God; Christ, embodiment of all Holy Mystery; Christ, in whom opposites are wed; Christ, who in me, when I am most myself, is WomanChrist.

Even in darkness at the edges of all the worlds, this One I See. This One I Love.

THE NEEDFUL TRUTH

The vision we hold of God becomes incarnated in the world we create. But we have kept our vision to ourselves; many have become blind. We have lived too long in a patriarchal vision. We have protected the fathers and sons from disillusionment. We have lied to the mothers to protect them from grief at the loss of their original truth. We have denied what we see in favor of their illusions. We have "silenced the savage music." So our collective vision of God became emptied of the reality only we could have seen. And when God becomes a mockery, the world loses its soul.

Leslie called yesterday. "I am trying to tell the truth," she said. "But I have denied it for so long that I have to be quick or it escapes me before I recognize it. I cover it up.

"I went into this day care center I needed to visit as part of the educational program I am in, and I saw immediately that it was really inferior. But instead of admitting to myself, 'There is something wrong here—the children are unhappy, the staff is bored and not involved, safety is being jeopardized, there is no creative stimulation,' I went into high gear. I really worked. And by the time I left the children were laughing and active, and the staff had lots of energy and ideas. I walked out smiling and saying to myself, 'Now *that* is a really good day care center!' But it wasn't. It wasn't, and I couldn't admit it. It was as if nothing *could* be wrong because nothing was supposed to be wrong. If I found something wrong, then it must be *my* fault. So I couldn't permit myself to even *see* the defects.

"I've thought and thought about that, and you know what? I act that way consistently. My marriage, my parenting, my social and religious life—I never permit myself to admit to anything being wrong. I've gotten so I barely notice—I just flow in and fix it. If it can't be fixed I deny it or blame myself.

"I must begin to tell the truth. Life depends upon it."

"What do you think of the Christ? Whose son is he?" This is the pivotal question of the Gospels. We know Peter's answer. But our own answer is left up to us. Those of us who tenaciously cling both to the Christian Gospels and to our experience of women's mysteries, we who want to reconcile these two visions, are confronted with a profound task. Both the militant Christians and the militant feminists reject us as heretical.

Here is the task: to tell the truth about opposites. To contain and be contained by the most profound paradox and to affirm the truth of both sides. If I find it impossible, something is being omitted from my vision or I am trying to live according to a lie. If I am a Christian and deny my vision of the Divine Feminine, I live an illusion. If I embody the Goddess but deny that I incarnate the Christ, I live an illusion. They do not meld, nor dovetail; they stand as opposites, but together—united. When our vision of Christ is separated from our vision of Divine Feminine Wisdom, what we see is "anti-Christ"; what we incarnate is destruction.

What has been torn must be healed. The truth must be seen. Its savage music must be sung. The illusive lies afflicting our vision of the Christ must be faced and uncovered if the sin of dualism is ever to be redeemed. We are the seers. We stand at the threshold.

WOMANCHRIST VISIONQUEST

The vision lies in our hearts, the truth in the dust at our feet. When we ask, "Where can I look to see what is needful?" the answer is "Here." To the question, "Who is the Christ," the answer is "One."

The quest is to live the most radical truth we can see. Trust no reality divided within itself. Patriarchy, which governs by division and domination by those perceived powerful over those perceived weak, is the "sin of the world" of which Jesus spoke. The truth is, we are not of that world. He was not of that world. Where Christianity is subjected to such a patriarchal system the religion that results is not of Christ. Where the scriptures promote domination and power-over they are not the revelation of God.

War in the name of Christ is blasphemy. Building better bombs to protect our "nation under God" from the "evil of communism" is blasphemy. Proclaiming "in God we trust" while the majority of people go hungry is blasphemy. Treating earth and her creatures mechanistically is blasphemy. Saying "God's in his heaven, all's right with the world," is blasphemy. Denying my own vision and accepting that my father-husband-son is the only image of God is blasphemy. Giving energy to systems of domination in the name of faith is blasphemy.

Look at the tangle of power in which our world is caught, struggling, nearly hoping to die. What monstrous god have we envisioned over the centuries to incarnate such evil in our lives? Dare we call this monster Christ?

I will not.

Christ is the One who stands in the darkness just over the threshold of our divisions. It is up to us to dare to be seers. What we envision is what we will become.

Let her speak, the woman within, the woman at the threshold, the woman who sees into the dark, into the core, into the primal untorn places. Let her tell the truth of her vision. Ask her the fundamental question: "What do you say of the Christ? Whose child is he?"

WHITE SHELL WOMAN SPEAKS

I am the ocean of life where the Christ rides the waves of my cosmic womb, growing, growing. I am woman pregnant with the future. I am woman nurturing the Holy Power of Life. I am woman preparing the egg of hope. In me is the Beginning and the End. Hidden in my wet folds shines the Eternal Pearl.

The Christ who is birthing in me will bring moist greening to the earth, will not fear the dark loam where the buried seed bursts.

Christ of love and the intense power of eros, I birth you.

Christ of tears for all who are frightened, who are diseased, who are tired of struggling, who blind themselves to possibility, who harden against feeling, who have become rigid—holding themselves tight against the ebb and flow of life's tides, I birth you.

Christ of imagination, poet-Christ, artist-Christ, Christ who dances on the waves, Christ who sings to flowers and makes friends with birds, I birth you.

Christ who gazes at the moon, who feels the rhythm of cosmic cycles, who is drawn by the tides, I birth you.

Deep Christ,
Christ salty with Wisdom,
Creative Christ,
Christ from whom all are born in joy and to whom all return in peace,
Christ, world of tomorrow,
You are *my* Child.

BLACK ROCK WOMAN SPEAKS

I am Earth.

I am etched with memory from the beginning, from the original birthing, from the primal coming forth.

Christ is what is most ancient in me, my deepest rooted memory, the image of all that can become. Christ is my heart.

I heal whatever is torn.

I bring life from what is dead.

I devour evil and from its waste make mountains.

I am the flesh of God.

I am the Mother of all.

I cannot be manipulated for selfish ends; my nature must be respected. What seeks to destroy me ceases to exist.

I continue.

And the Christ is *my* Child.

RED ROSE WOMAN SPEAKS

I am one with the Fire.

I am one with the Blood.

I am passion and I am power

I am the courage to speak the truth, the daring to live justice.

I am beauty.

Christ, passionate for justice, compassionate with the oppressed, I see you in the fire.

Christ, walking the roads of the world, clasping our hands, creating a circle around the earth, I see you in the fire.

Christ, revealing that our power is within ourselves and among one another, teaching by your death that our power over one another kills the Divine Fire in us, I see you in the blood.

Christ birthing peace,
Christ walking away from war, from hierarchies of power,
Christ revealed in communities of compassion,
Christ, fullness of life, of love and of beauty,
Christ, incarnation of our best but most fragile dreams,
Christ of the New Earth,
You are *my* Child.

WIND SONG WOMAN SPEAKS

I sing the song and the dream,
I am woman of tomorrow,
I am secret of the wind.

Spirit woman, whisper woman, woman hidden where the leaves sing,
flicker woman, hummingbird woman, gull-cry woman, woman of breath,
falling-leaf woman, elusive woman, woman veiled with light, inspiration
woman, mind woman, woman of ideas, woman with plans, crying woman,
keening woman, screeching woman, screaming woman, laughing woman,
nightingale woman, lark woman, whistling woman, woman moaning in
love, woman groaning in labor, woman wailing in death, ecstatic woman,
sound woman, singing woman, singing woman, singing woman.

Christ is my song.
Christ will not be silenced.
Christ is *my* Child.

TEARS: BLESSED ARE THOSE WHO SUFFER PERSECUTION FOR JUSTICE'S SAKE

"If the world hates you," said Jesus of the patriarchal
world into which he was born, which he attempted to influence to
see a different vision, and because of which he was put to death,
"remember that it hated me before you . . . if they persecuted me,
they will persecute you too" (John 15:18, 20).

As we read on in the Gospel of John we discover that the source of this patriarchal world's hatred was its emptiness of "truth" and the consequent failure to comprehend the essential oneness of reality: the divine with the human in the wholeness of creation brought to fullness in the Incarnation of the Christ. The divisions characteristic of "the world" resulted in a hatred so strong that Jesus warns his friends, "the time is coming when anyone who kills you will think he is doing a holy duty for God" (John 16:2).

The sign of God is oneness, a reweaving of the fabric of creation, a universalization of Incarnation. The "truth" is that we are one. Truth, consequently, results in love and compassion for all that is. Jesus prays:

> "I passed your word on to them,
> and the world hated them,
> because they belong to the world
> no more than I belong to the world. (John 17:14)

> Consecrate them in the truth;
> Your word is truth. (John 17:16)

> May they all be one.
> [Abba] may they be one in us,
> as you are in me and I am in you,
> so that the world may believe it was you who sent me.
> I have given them the glory you gave to me
> that they may be one as we are one.
> With me in them and you in me,
> may they be so completely one
> that the world will realize it was you who sent me.
> (John 17:21–23)

Where can we find this Christ-vision now, I wonder as I hurry through the rain down the hill from the torn oak. Where can we find it *lived*? I know this: I often feel lonely for One I have sought in every community to which I have belonged. I often feel lonely for One whom I only glimpse through the tears of our fragmented human efforts toward a reconciled community of compassion.

We have much to heal, much that is torn to reweave, much that is alienated to embrace. And in the process we have much to suffer.

Helen M. Luke reminds us, in her wise reflections on *Old Age,* that to suffer means "to bear" or "to carry," to be an "undercarriage," rather than to be "pressed down" (depression), or "struck down" (affliction), or "weighed down" (grief).*

Patriarchal persecution of women has often afflicted us, pressed us down, and caused us grief. In such pain there is no blessing. In such outrageous persecution as the burning of millions of women during the European witch-hunts—when the patriarchal church and state made real the prophecy of Jesus that "the time is coming when anyone who kills you will think he is doing a holy duty for God" (John 16:2)—there is no blessing. In the common afflictions of common women—insulted by ribald and trivializing jokes; brutalized by men who violate trust in the home, in the workplace, and on the streets; betrayed by other women whose minds and hearts have been torn by patriarchal power; restricted in the fulfillment of their destiny by laws that result from patriarchal interpretations of what that destiny ought to be—there is no blessing.

The blessing comes from *suffering* persecution for the sake of justice. We carry it. We bear it. It marks us like a scar. We feel the pain of it, but it does not weigh us down. We do not pretend it has not happened, does not happen, is not happening. We tell the truth about the persecution. We carry it. We let it mark us, we get to know it so well that we can feel its most subtle stirrings both within ourselves and in all our relationships. We let our knowledge of it move us to the edge, to the threshold. We touch where the world is torn; we feel each jagged line of terror. We suffer this so we will not forget, so we will know the lies, so we can bear new life and not give it away to delusion again.

We suffer so we can be present at this birthing—awake, participating, aware. We are mothers of Justice. We are midwives to one another in the birthing of WomanChrist.

Last night in a dream I was leaving my home of many years. With me I could take only as much as I could carry. Standing in the center of a large room filled with my lifelong collection of books, I pon-

---

* Helen M. Luke, *Old Age* (New York: Parabola Books, 1987).

dered which ones to take and which ones to leave behind. A threshold dream. How can I know what I need if I cannot see what I will encounter?

Women and men stand together at a threshold of unknowing. We need to bring into the future from the past only what gives life and can make us whole again. Out of the patriarchal persecution we have suffered for thousands of years, and which has left us torn, we have learned some truth about life and spirituality. This truth we carry over the threshold. This truth is the "savage music [our] golden mouths are sworn to utter."

SAVAGE MUSIC

What we have called God, Goddess, the Holy One, the Divine, and so many other names throughout the eons, in evolutions of cultures since the Stone Age is a mystery beyond our capacity to name, define, or image. All language or image referring to this Mystery is metaphor.

Human experience of this "God-Mystery" results from an interpretation we place upon our consciousness of being/becoming.

The most vital source of the "God-experience" is one's personal being/becoming.

A woman's or man's "God-experience" is mediated through woman-nature or man-nature, respectively.

Creation is the process by which God becomes embodied.

Incarnation is full consciousness of our creation. Jesus, who is called the Christ, embodies this full consciousness for the Christian.

Christian life is the process of Incarnation in each individual, in each community, and in the world.

Only where the church is an Incarnational community is it Christian.

Dualism, which splits creation and sets up hierarchies of domination, is anti-Incarnational.

Patriarchy, of which dualism is a fundamental operative principle, is anti-Incarnational and not Christian.

Where the church is patriarchal and dualistic, it is not Christian.

Scripture, when it is an articulation of a patriarchal church, contains only remnants of Christian belief.

One task of Christians today is to sort through what we have called "Christian scriptures and traditions" in order to differentiate between what is Christian and what is patriarchal.

WomanChrist spirituality is a process of Incarnation as experienced through woman-nature.

WomanChrist spirituality is necessary, especially now, because the experience of the "God-Mystery" mediated through women and through expression of the feminine energies in men has been greatly suppressed, discredited, trivialized, and feared by patriarchy for thousands of years. So long as Incarnation in woman-nature is suppressed or denied there can be no true Christianity, nor fullness of creation, nor adequate metaphor for God.

VISIONS, NOT TEARS

Who we shall become we are already in our souls. How poignant of Jesus to leave us with suffering as the final blessing. How mysterious. How paradoxical. How true to life. But never again the victimizing pain. Never again the oppression of accepted domination. Never again self-pity. Instead we suffer to bring truth, justice, and life. This truth we will carry: that in us opposites are joined, the wound is healed, the torn oak flowers.

What is birthing is within. Each moment, with each thought, in each choice of each person who believes, the opposites are joined, the wound is healed, the torn oak flowers.

> We who stand at the threshold
> Peering into the dark,
> Offering the shell, the rock, the flower, and the song,
> We who suffer the persecutions of the centuries,
> > to remember,
> > to transform,
> > to learn compassion,
> > to give birth,
> We bear Justice like a silver bird in our wombs;
> And she will be born.
> And she will fly before us as blessing
> Into the unknown.
> And we will follow
> Seeing.